ZOETIC SOUL

Pertaining To Life. Your Life

Jan Mayfield

Copyright © 2016 by Jan Mayfield

Published by Conscious Dreams Publishing

ZOETIC SOUL

Pertaining To Life. Your Life.

The original work of author Jan Mayfield

Text design – Jan Mayfield

Editing – Daniella Blechner

Cover created by Kera Robson/Jan Mayfield

Publisher - Conscious Dreams Publishing

Copyright notice

All rights reserved. No part of this publication may be reproduced, stored in a retrieval system, or transmitted, in any form or by any means, without the prior written permission of the publisher, nor be otherwise circulated in any form of binding or cover other than that in which it is published and without a similar condition being imposed on the subsequent purchaser. The information in this book should not be treated as a substitute for professional medical advice. All use of the information given in this book is at the reader's discretion. The Author or Publisher is not responsible for your interpretations.

ISBN 978-0-9955712-1-1

Year published 2017

Jan Mayfield

Zen
Oasis
Evolving
Time
In
Consciousness

Seek
Out
Universal
Life

CONTENTS

Preface	v
Chapter 1 - How Did I Arrive Here?	01
Chapter 2 - A to B and Pre-A	12
Chapter 3 - What Is Trance?	47
Chapter 4 - Suicide Passings	53
Chapter 5 - Trancing Deeper Into The Universal Energies	168
Chapter 6 - As One Chapter Closes, Another Door Opens	253
Chapter 7 - Trancing Life's Universal Energies	271
Chapter 8 - And Finally, Before You Transform	469
Acknowledgements	480
About The Author	482

Preface

Zoetic Soul was born out of my passion for all things spiritual, my soul's direction and a desire to enable others to live in their soul's intended and miraculous way.

It has taken 18 months from start to finish. My life as a medium led me to learn how to trance souls' voices. But it was the readings I gave to people that led to me writing this book. Or was it? Was it that I was guided to write? Was it that I recognised all the clues on my life path, grabbed them and made my soul fulfilled? What was it? You can decide.

You can make those decisions in your life too. *Zoetic Soul* will take you on a journey that will become your journey. Tranced are the voices of souls who wish to communicate information to assist you in living a more purposeful and fulfilling life. *Zoetic Soul* is full of subliminal ideas and guidance to enable a crystal clear vision. Absorb the matter and the guidance will follow.

This book will be many things to many people; read and you will soon discover that it actually takes very little to let go of the conditioning embedded in us from birth. See how yours drops away as you release your soul's armour to reveal...

There are no major declarations, no magical secrets or embellished trivialities to live in this way. Preparing your earth to fertilise your seeds is all that is required.

On all the proofreads, there were tears, Ah-ha! moments, lost times of reflection and realisations that we can create our own soul fulfilment.

Zoetic Soul is designed for you to make changes in your life now. You know there is something missing and you need guidance. *Zoetic Soul* is that guidance.

Read through at your own pace, but you may want to linger on some chapters longer than others. Purchase a new notebook to journal your poignant moments.

■ ■ ■

Jan Mayfield

<u>Chapter 1</u>

HOW DID I ARRIVE HERE?
Looking At The Events That Guided Me To Write This Book

∞ ∞ ∞

The Events That Led To This Day

Over the years, as with most people, pivotal moments, occurrences and events happen and we just take them for granted. We very rarely tend to look beyond the surface of most situations. Once I started doing readings and my psychic mediumship work full time, I was guided to look deeper into the how's and why's. It was, of course, spirit showing me; I use the term 'spirit' to account for a being that is no longer living in an earthly body.

I am a Psychic Medium and Universal-Energy Healer. I do see into the future and can connect to the souls of those who have passed from their earthly bodies. There are many other sides to my work; without listing everything, all you need to know is everything is on a spiritual level, but I am different.

It was my grandma's 100th birthday that brought on the latest major changes in my life. We were having a family and close friends gathering for her special day. Her home was a room in a nursing home for the elderly. A really innocent comment was made by me that angered a relative; this led to her shouting and blaming me for the whole world going wrong. I would not react because it was my dear grandma's birthday. I loved her more than anything, and over the years we had created a very special bond.

To this day I do not understand why this happened, but it led to this person totally cutting me out of their life. I knew I could not react; I had messages and words of encouragement coming into my head through the whole process. They were from spirit, whom I trust, believe and have faith in, so I knew it was meant to be happening. Thankfully, other family members heard and stood there with their jaws dropped at what they had witnessed. Except for one and that did not surprise me as it had happened this way since she was born.

Time went on and as I continued with my readings and connecting to spirit through meditation, I increasingly noticed that I was telling people about A to B. A to B is the process of life and death; A you are born and B you pass over out of your earthly body. Briefly, I was telling them about their life, that it is theirs and what others do is not for them to understand, just to accept. I could see that people were responding to this way of thinking; it gave them another angle on their situations.

You are you, with your choices of how to live, feel and be. The penny started to drop; I had to do this with my family member. I sent a card to them, where I clearly stated that there was no excuse for their behaviour and wished them well as I wanted to keep it light.

This was not received well. Through a third-party family member, I was given a few pages of A4 from her to read stating all the things that I had done wrong in my life including her perception of me- which was exactly that; her perception. I cannot deny that this upset me, and the tears rolled as I sobbed for a while. As the tears changed to anger, I ripped up then burnt the paper and flushed it down the toilet. I knew then that I would move on.

The theory in ripping up the paper is to let go. A great way to exercise this is to write down any issues that are holding you back in life and rip up the paper. In this case, although I had it written for me, the action of ripping it up invoked anger and tears, thus a letting go. If there are issues in your life, I strongly urge you to write it, rip it up, burn it, and let it go.

The burning or cremation is the end of the issues.

I like to take it to the next stage by flushing the remains down the toilet. All thoughts and connections, if there are any left, go right down the pan, pipe work and out into the ocean. Therefore, for me, the person that wrote it and the words on the paper cannot be read, as they are both in the middle of the ocean. I have no memory of a single word on that paper.

Look into the crystal clear, fresh, cleansing water; there is nothing but water!

I always asked how my estranged family member was, but as time passed X did not want to tell me; her words were that she felt awkward. Strange, really, as this was supposed to be the matriarch who was now pushing me further away from the family.

Life continued and as it did, I kept getting more information on the A to B process and used it a lot in my readings. Feedback reassured me, as many who came to me for personal and business readings described how it helped them tremendously. Some even had life changing moments. I knew what I was saying was helping. That is my work: to help, guide, educate and deliver. In my readings and meditations, I was also told about Pre-A; this is the time before you are born into an earthly body.

Life went on and my grandma seemed to go downhill after her birthday so I visited as often as I could and would give her spiritual healing, which is a beautiful energy that comes from source to the person though your hands and thoughts. Many people also train in

Reiki, as did I to Master Teacher level. This type of healing is said to balance the body and I feel aids transition. She liked it when I put my hand on her forehead and stroked her head. On all my visits, especially as she declined, I was given visions and I could see other spirits in the room with us. It was the most amazing experience for me; I did and still do feel very privileged to have experienced those out-of-this-world visions. Other people would visit and I would always step back from her bed and give them the option to get close to her, and to experience that most precious feeling.

In the two to three weeks before her passing, her progressively rapid decline was obvious. Every evening I would sit next to her as the staff popped in and out of the room; there were other visitors who always left around eight o'clock, but I stayed until eleven o'clock each time.

On more than one occasion, the staff asked me what time I was leaving. I felt like someone was making sure I would be there all evening, call it a gut feeling or intuition. The other visitors said their goodbyes and told me not to stay too late.

I read to her; she liked me to read from the book of Corinthians and I had some poems I knew she would like and a few prayers too. Sometimes I would just sit still by her bedside and watch the activity from the spirits in the room. I remember one night seeing angels come down around her stomach area and just hover around. The only way I can describe this is as if it was like they were untying something from that area of her body; it was a beautiful serene experience for me, and Grannie Mary looked peaceful. I felt so humble and privileged to witness this. Everyone called her Grannie Mary.

That evening the staffed popped in and out as usual. There was one member of staff who I really gelled with and I knew she thought a lot of Grannie Mary. As the time ticked by, her deterioration was obvious; she was eerily calm and still took shallow, gasping breaths. I was giving her healing and stroking her head very gently to assist her transition. There are no words to say how beautiful this experience was for me and I know I was supposed to be there. She remained at peace and took her last breath at 11.01pm.

The following led to using the Pre-A and A to B more in my own life, and spirit gave me extra information on this. In private sessions I used it and I also tested it for myself.

In a million years I would never envisioned the following events that totally changed my life…

I visited family members the day following Grannie Mary's transition and asked if I could be of help. I drove them round to the usual places to register the death, I helped with official documentations and made phone calls. On one of the days, we were reminiscing about Grannie Mary and her life.

One of my family members stared at me and venomously said…

"You made us feel really uncomfortable when you were holding her and stroking her head."

Knock me down with a feather! What? Where did that come from?

Now, this did upset me. I love my grandma more than a sister, aunt, mother, grandmother, and best friend; she was and still is all of those and more rolled into one. No one can take our love for each other away.

I will just mention that I was always the "black sheep" in the family and was called it on numerous occasions by more than one family member. *You are different, not the same as us*.

It is all right for you, an Aunt once said to me when we were talking about her daughter's marriage breakup.

What is all right for me?

Well, you can deal with everything!

She said this as though I had no emotions. Is that how they saw me? I could hear it over and over in my head, until the day I chose to embrace being the black sheep; who wants to be the same as anyone else anyway?

I was healing Grannie Mary, helping her in her transition and when those family members came into the room, I always stood up and asked if they wanted the seat I was sitting in. On occasions, the seat would be left empty because they did not want to sit so close.

I felt like I had been punched in the gut. I knew this was not right and I was trying to read the situation and listen to the messages in my head. They meant this. It was not said on a whim. One of them then said she knew how much I loved her.

Was it wrong to love my Grannie Mary?

Or was it that she could not love her?

Not ONCE did they ask if I was alright, or how I felt all the way through her decline, not once. But it did not matter because my beliefs take me beyond someone else's interpretation of me. What I did find strange was the insecurities about me being close to and loving my grandma.

After reading the sheets of A4 from the family member I spoke about earlier, I realised that if she thought the words were true, her whole life had been a lie. Most of the words were not true. Just her perception of me.

In my life and with readings and helping others in situations like this I always suggest they imagine a mirror in front of the person's face. The words are actually for the person writing them; they just don't know how to deal with their life and it should be reflected back.

What made it worse was the family member who was uncomfortable with me loving my grandma, would not and did not want to listen to my replies or comments to these sheets of A4. Why? Because I am the black sheep and should take everything the others give me.

Now the voices from spirit are loud in my head.

"Do it, say it now and we will help you." Oh my goodness, I opened my mouth and all these words came out; I was shaking too. I would never have envisioned speaking in this way to these people. But it was because I had held back that I was letting it go now… whooo hoooo, how good did I feel afterwards? A few days later I began to realise that I had released the conditioned black sheep within me... Oh, I laugh so loud as I type this because I have seen the light!

I thought Grannie Mary's funeral would be awkward; it was a little, but the only people that did not speak to me were the three of them. Everyone else hugged me for me. I read a verse to Grannie Mary as her carcass lay in the coffin and her soul danced around the chapel because it was right for me to do so. I celebrate her passing and thank her for working with me from the other side.

I tried to make amends with two of the family members, or at least bring back communication for the sake of my daughters, granddaughters and niece. But it was not meant to be and I stopped. I cannot change the way they perceive me.

My life has taken the most incredible steps since being released. I was never meant to be caged by their conditioning and beliefs.

■ ■ ■

Chapter 2

A TO B AND PRE-A

Working Through The Time Before You Are Born, Your Life Line And Beyond

∞ ∞ ∞

A to B and Pre-A
What's It All About?

First and foremost, what you will read on the following pages is a methodology that has been developed over a number of years with many clients. Working closely with them, I have been able to monitor the changes in their lives. The constant changes confirmed that this thinking methodology/concept can and will change your life. However, as with every other concept YOU have to do the work to make it happen in the first place, and you have to want the changes. Make that decision and it will become part of your daily thinking.

The facts are everyone is BORN INTO and everyone PASSES OUT OF THEIR EARTHLY BODY. I will refer A as born and B as passes over. I am introducing Pre-A; this is the time before your soul enters an earthly body. As you read about Pre-A, it is important to remember that at this point you are not in a human body with feelings and emotions. You are in the time before birth, planning what to experience.

A=BORN
B=PASSES OVER

Pre-A=BEFORE YOU ARE BORN

What happens in between A and B?

Pre-A - - - - - - - - A-BORN - - - - - - - - your life - - - - - - - - - B-PASSES OVER

This is your life path, and what you do in it is your choice. Or is it?

Everyone's beliefs will vary according to conditioning, parents, family, schooling, friends, society and events. Everyone's life path is predestined, but with free will you can change it to a certain degree. Or can you?

This book is written from my experiences with readings, guidance and intuitive coaching sessions with people who have contacted me. My sessions are always given with a connection to spirit, as it is their voice that gives me the words to say to clients. Therefore, this book has been delivered from spirit.

As a psychic medium, I am given information in many forms from spirit, and it is always relevant to the situation or person that I am working with. My whole life is this way; I live in the most divinely guided way possible. But I still have to make decisions, and I have the ability to make choices with opportunities as they present themselves. I have to recognise them and act accordingly. Examples throughout the book will demonstrate this.

Emotions play a huge part in our lives. Life without emotions would be easy but who wants to be a robot without feelings and emotions?

There are many gurus who have studied and written in great detail about the spirit world, pure spirits, certain secrets, and journeys in life. All of these are relevant through time; the need to be dynamic in this ever evolving world is necessary.

The right teacher/guide/coach will find you when the time is right, and their words will resonate in their unique way.

This concept is something that everyone can be comfortable with and you will make the decision on the timing for you.

The following is an example of Pre-A. There are very few people who remember Pre-A in their earthly life.

Please read with an open mind as it will all make sense the further we go.

I believe that we are pure souls who continue to live in another part of the universe, if we are not on earth. We all have a spirit family or spirit group which we leave to come into an earthly body. On earth, we learn life skills and have experiences to further enlighten the soul.

In conjunction with a higher source, we decide on what we, the soul, want to learn/experience on any given placement on earth. This is what I call **Pre-A**; you are not born at this point.

Divine Source is a general term for the soul who speaks to you at Pre-A. Your own belief system may use another word here.

I will refer to **Divine Source** as **DS** and **Soul** as **S.**

■ ■ ■

Dialogue

In earthly language, the dialogue may go something like this between Divine Source and Soul.

DS: Good morning Soul, how are you today?

S: Very well, thank you. I have been thinking that I might like to visit earth.

DS: We can look at the lessons/experiences/learnings you need to have at this incarnation.

S: We can, and I would like to do this in the near future. Soul makes a list of everything it knows it has not experienced.

- To be born by C-section
- To a mother who drinks alcohol
- A father who works away and is very busy
- To have an elder sister
- To have a rare childhood illness
- To have the most loving and kind grandparents
- To learn patience
- To learn to believe in self
- To fall in love
- To meet a person from a past life
- To be abusive and bully other people

- To study hard
- To work and have a job
- To marry twice
- To have psychic abilities
- To see spirits
- To be pregnant twice
- To have one child
- To know their life purpose
- To die, but with regrets, peacefully
- Learn to trust
- Learn patience
- Learn self-belief
- Let go of fear

DS: Thank you, Soul, for your list. Let's look at it together; come sit with me.

S: What do you think?

DS: This is a good list of experiences for you.

Life is not about having the experiences alone, it is looking at how you contend with, deliver, change and come through each one. Emotional ties and the releasing of them to enable in-the-moment experiences to take place, will lead to soul fulfilment.

DS: looking at your previous incarnations, we will determine your experiences required this time.

S: I am excited for my next incarnation.

■ ■ ■

Think about it...

You may want to stop for a few minutes and think about your life.

How has it been?

What have you experienced?

What comes into your mind when I ask those questions?

On the following page is an exercise for you to work through.

A bad relationship in the past may lead to you repeating that type of relationship in the future, even though you thought you had ended it.

It is not enough to end something; we have to let go of the emotion attached to it. To correct this early on will enable less repetitions.

You may have heard people saying or even said to yourself:

"Why do I pick the same type of partner again and again?"

"Why do I keep getting...?"

"I should have learned my lesson by now."

"Will I ever learn?"

These and many more statements are all said because YOU are repeating and not learning. If the lesson was learned correctly and the emotional tie released, then you would move on.

However much this angers you, you will see a pattern and it is only YOU that can control this. Jot down everything else that comes into your head right now. You may fill a page with random words.

You should begin to experience Ah-ha! moments as you recognise your past in present situations.

As you continue to read this book, you will have more moments that resonate in your life now.

■ ■ ■

Exercise

Take some time out to think about the following questions.

There is no right or wrong, everything is personal to you.

Think about your life and write a little for each question, be honest with yourself.

As you begin to think about your childhood where do you first feel?

(It may be your head, belly, heart or somewhere else on your body.)

_____

As you being to think about your teenage years, where do you feel?

(It may be your head, belly, heart or somewhere else on your body.)

_____

As you think about your adult life, what holds you back?

(for example, fear, lack of self-worth, lack of confidence.)

_____

Do you have the same feelings connecting adult life to teenage and childhood? Name one or two

_____

Do you see how life joins us to our thoughts, conditioning and past experiences?

_____

You can now feel very proud that you have recognised this in your life. Be positive and know you can let go of the past conditioning and move forward.

As you read further, it is a good idea to repeat this exercise and see how your answers have changed.

Pre-A

Today is the day to be conceived. You have chosen your parents and created and established experiences and lessons to be learnt in dialogue with DS.

Your mother and father to be are trying for a baby.

You are conceived.

The womb is your comfort for the next 9 months or so.

You feel happy, warm and content. But you have no recollection of your life as that beautiful soul in spirit world. Those memories are erased at conception/birth.

Whilst in the womb, you can hear the outside world: people singing, music playing, people talking, traffic and all the normal events that are going on around us.

Close your eyes for a moment and imagine you are in the womb. What can you hear?

One day you hear crying and shouting, very close to you, but don't know who it is. You hear more crying and then some laughter. You don't know what this is. You can feel pressure as the area above you (Mother's stomach) is pressed and you feel anxious but, don't know what 'anxious' is. You hear voices that are strong and again a woman crying. She is told to come back every week to be monitored.

You settle back down in the comfort of the womb.

Over the coming months you hear arguing, crying and shouting.

A strong sense of being pulled in a downward motion and it does not feel right. You hear panic, shouting and lots of commotion.

"It's a girl," you hear someone say, "C-section was the only way, the feet were stuck."

Not knowing what has happened you feel confused, disorientated and alone. You know that you did not make it out on your own.

You hear the crying again, but now you see the eyes of the crying woman. She smiles as she cries. You feel warmth and love. You want to snuggle your birth mother.

What now? You are snatched from the crying eyes that feel love. Lots more commotion, then you take a breath that is…

"Is it my last breath?"

They pump your chest with the ends of their big fingers as you watch from above.

"What are they doing?"

"Shall I go back?"

They all step away and breathe a sigh of relief, as they see you return to continue your earthly life. You see the crying eyes.

There are many voices talking to the crying eyes. You hear them say that your heart is broken and you will need operations over the coming years. Right now you are cuddled by the crying eyes.

You have now achieved three of your life lessons/experiences. One being born by C-section and the other I feel will be the heart condition, as a rare childhood illness which will manifest over the coming years.

This is Pre-A completed. You did not turn back, and many people believe that there is a moment before or at actual birth that you as a Pre-A have a choice to go back to the spirit world.

■ ■ ■

Miscarriage

On numerous occasions, when I am giving readings, I am shown that it is the choice of the foetus/Pre-A to go back to the spirit world.

In this scenario the mother would have asked at Pre-A to experience miscarriage and the foetus would have asked not to be born this time.

I am shown that EVERYONE has their own Pre-A and it is their purpose to live this. We have to realise we have very little or no actual control over some things happening in life.

This life is not easy and it is ongoing eternally.

Everyone in your earthy family will have their own Pre-A and not everyone in your earthly family is in your spirit family.

Living within your own A to B will allow you to be in that wonderful place of self-love and self-belief. Allowing others to cross into your A to B will cause frustration and disharmony in your life. It is you and your perception that will alter here. More about that later.

■ ■ ■

"The Womb" is a verse I wrote; you can hear it being read on YouTube on my channel, Jan Mayfield. Channelled from Isaac.

The Womb

I see my life before, I see as I am engulfed by the watery love of the womb I think, I know, I remember.

I develop in the watery love of the womb.

I hear the sounds, noise and vibrations raised with anger.

I hear the voices.

Man and woman unharmoniously creating unseen futuristic psychological disturbance as I lay in the watery womb.

I grow and develop, I am shaken, I bang against the watery side of the womb. I am thrown from one side to another. Bang.

Bang, I am stunned in the watery womb of anger and hate. I am out of control; I fear the anger as it rises outside the watery womb

Where is the love? Where is it?

Nine months now I resist the pull to the fear and anger. I resist.

Two weeks I hear them say, we then shall cut the baby out!

Anger and shouting, hurting me now as I push and push

This journey is not smooth; I am stuck in the watery womb.

I am stuck.

Help me, help me as I fear the passage to contentment and love. I fear. I breathe and smell the fear within.

I see a bright light, a white light of love; I decide to go to the light.

To earth, I cannot go to the fear and anger they created. I go back home to the love and light.

They say I am born still...

■ ■ ■

You Are Born Birth To 7 Years

We are looking at the poignant points throughout the first 7 years of life. Keep in mind the dialogue that was made with DS. Your dialogue is somewhere inside your memory, in your subconscious, and will resurface now and again. These may be déjà vu moments.

Recognition is key to reaching, surmounting and learning from everything in the dialogue box. This, in turn, will enable you to be the person you chose to be.

As you read through, you will begin to see how events that happened in the womb will have an effect on you in your growing years.

Born into the world a babe in arms and ready to take on the world as YOU.

Wait! You are not YOU; they give you a name. What is this Jasmine? Jasmine is my name. I am not YOU. I am Jasmine. This is a recount of Jasmine's formative years. Jasmine is a fictional character I have used here as an example.

■ ■ ■

As You Grow- 1 Year

Small and crying, I am being fed and not much else going on in my little world.

I begin to hear the crying that I heard in the womb and the shouting and arguing, too.

I hear the words of people speaking.

"She may experience strange sensations in the chest, which will lead to monthly check-ups at the hospital."

The doctors say they need to keep a close eye on me for 18 months, and at that point further discussions will take place.

Happy times are also experienced; a birthday, Christmas, and a holiday with the old ones, **grandparents**. I see no tears and hear no arguing with my **grandparents**. These wonderful people generate **beautiful love**. I spend lots of time with them.

■ ■ ■

As You Grow- 2 Years

I witness the crying and arguing in the home, but who would I be to question, as it is normal. My **sister**, who is older, is a little cruel and she teaches naughty words as I begin to speak. When I repeat them, I am **shouted** at and sometimes given a sharp **slap**. Just like Dad to Mum.

A check up at the hospital, as they don't want to miss anything within my development that might make my heart stop again. It is a **rare condition;** nothing can be done and it might never happen again.

"My heart might never stop again, but my heart might stop again."

I repeat these words over and over in my mind.

"I might die."

Time spent with my grandparents over this last year led to such happy emotions. I love my grandma so much; she is in my heart all the time, with such warmth. I have a beautiful feeling being around her. She hugs me tight too.

■ ■ ■

As You Grow- 3 Years

Everything is going black; something is not right... I am going... I am going...

"I can't see."

"Where am I going?" I ask myself.

I see a beautiful white light. I see my mother picking me up out of my bed. I am floating up in the sky, I am high above. I see her carry me down stairs, through the door and into an ambulance with flashing lights.

They press my chest again. I hear crying, I hear the sirens as the ambulance speeds through the streets, and I see the blue shadows on the wet ground as I observe from above. We reach the large building, where people rush out to greet us.

"Hello!" I say

I am not there, I am here.

"Hello, can you see me?"

You can't see me.

I am not to be seen.

They keep pressing my chest, rushing around and looking at each other with wide eyes.

What are they doing?

I look at the light, the bright white light and see my spirit family; they look so happy and inviting but they tell me I have to return to my body. That earthly vehicle that I chose.

One last pump on my chest and in I go, I am sucked into my body with force so sudden I almost jump off the bed. That is what you would call a near death experience. But it was not my time to go.

As I got to this part of the book I was wondering if I was on the right track. Being the spiritual person I am, one night I asked the angels and all my spirits to give me a sign.

A couple of days later my phone rang...

"Hello, Jan speaking..."

The lady on the phone was crying, and very distraught. She asked for guidance and some form of hope as her 2-week old baby girl was on life support, and the consultants had told her she would not survive. I could hear the desperation in her voice.

In this type of work, you HAVE to listen to spirit and on no occasion should you be guided by your own perception, beliefs or understandings. You have to be guided by spirit. And this, I do always. So I asked spirit what they wanted me to say to this lady.

Well, they did not show me the baby passing over; what they showed me was so beautiful. I could see the lady's grandmother, the baby's great grandmother, as a spirit. She showed me divine healing to the baby. She cupped the baby's head in her hands and I could see pure white light going into the baby from the head to the bottom of her feet. This was so special to me, and I knew that spirits were there looking after the baby. I was shown she would move her legs as she lay in the incubator.

Well the mum gasped, as she had just been with her minutes before and her daughter had moved her legs and feet. I could then see the baby's eyes were closed, but her eyeballs were moving under her eyelids; spirit said to tell her to look out for this happening.

I also saw a child at the bottom of the cot holding her feet and was told it was the lady's son, who was miscarried in the month of July. She confirmed the miscarriage in July. The Grandmother and son were there with the baby.

We continued to talk about more general things that were going on; she was telling me how the consultants were talking over the baby in a very negative way and she did not like this, because she believed the baby would hear and it could affect her future recovery.

I truly believe this, too.

This was the confirmation I had asked for. Thank you, universe. I am unaware of the baby's condition. If I find out before finishing this book I will make a point of telling you all. I feel the baby is special and is here for Mum.

■ ■ ■

As You Grow- 4 Years

Always around, watching and telling me to do this and not to do that. *You are ill, you might die*; those are the words I continually hear from my mother.

My grandmother is taking me to preschool; it is my first day. I walk tall and proud as she holds my hand. Just me and her.

I overhear the teacher talking to my grandmother. My mother had previously spoken to her about my illness. I wonder what illness, as the doctors have said I am recovered. Mother informed the teacher that I must not run around too much; physical exertion is out of the question. I might die. I hear those words. I might die.

As I sit on the carpet for reading time, a lady appears in the doorway; she looks at me and smiles then goes away. I cannot see her now. I wonder if anyone else saw her. As I look around the room, everyone else is looking at the teacher.

I love story time. I imagine that I am the character in the book. I dream and have wonderful visions, and imagery comes into my mind's eye as the book is read to the class. Sometimes I close my eyes.

I open my eyes and see the lady smiling at me again, and I smile back this time. The teacher notices and glances towards the door, then back at me. There is no one there again. I like the old lady by the door. I have seen her before when I was watching the ambulance.

After the first day at school, my mother collects me. I am a little disappointed not to see my grandmother's smiling face when we are told it was home time. My mother and I walk back home; she doesn't ask about my day, though. She is only concerned that I had not run around... *You know you could die if you do.*

We arrive at home, and mum grips my hand tightly. I know my father is home as I hear noises in the kitchen. He is loud. He shouts at my mother. She rushes around to help him. She does everything he tells her to do. I run to my room upstairs and listen.

He continues to shout the words that she is not good enough and she made me ill. He makes her to go to the shop to buy more drink. She has no money. He screeches at her to go and earn some.

I hear Mum close the door on her way out. A few hours later she comes back with drink and some food for us all to share. Father is happy now; he and Mother drink together. In my bed, I have the covers over my head as I hear the laughter turn to shouting. I press them to my ears as I hear slapping and crying. The laughter has gone. I sleep.

■ ■ ■

Jan Mayfield

As You Grow- 5 Years

It is my birthday and my father is not here. I can't recall him at any of my birthdays. For this birthday, I am allowed three school friends to join us for tea, and I am so excited. I am not allowed friends into the house on any other day.

In the kitchen, I watch as Mother prepares food but she does not realise I am there. I see her hand go into her apron pocket and she takes a drink from the little bottle she keeps hidden; she does this again and again. Tears fall out of her eyes and roll down her cheeks. She is crying. *Why does that drink make you cry?* I ask myself.

She looks across at me and like a dog shakes after being in water, she shakes herself as if to take away the tears. "Where is Father?" I ask, but she just shakes again. I think she shakes when she does not know what to say to me.

"He has to work. Come on now, your friends will be here soon." She ushers me out of the kitchen. "It is your Happy Birthday."

Oh, a wonderful sense of warmth is encasing me as the lady appears, the one that stands in the door smiling. She says everything will be alright and that she is here to look after me. She looks a little like my grandmother.

I hear someone knocking on the door, and I hear chattering too. Yippee! It is my friends. I feel safe now and ready to have my Happy Birthday.

They come in and we play games, we laugh, we eat the food, and we talk. Mother stands and watches and joins in sometimes, but lets us have fun on our own too. We are happy and she is smiling.

What a delightful day. I know I am growing up, I can feel it inside, but I do feel different somehow from how my friends are. I see different people to them. I know more. I see what happens before it comes on the news and I know what someone is going to say before they say it.

The other day, I was standing with Mother while she was chatting away with a friend of hers outside the shop. I stood looking at her and I could see what she was thinking and I had the words in my head before they came out of her mouth. I laughed and they both looked at me and wondered what I was laughing at. I just smiled because I saw the lady again, the one that looks like my grandmother. She just smiled at me and went away. *She is lovely,* I remember thinking, as I felt the warmth around me.

■ ■ ■

As You Grow- 6 Years

Summer has arrived and the birds are singing and chatting outside my window, which is open slightly. As the sun shines through the curtains, I watch the shadows dancing on my bed. I get up slowly and think about what we will do today at school. I feel happy and smile lots as I go and wash my face and clean my teeth.

Opening the door makes me realise that my father is back from his travels. I hear him speaking to my mother. He has raised his voice to her and I know.. I just know that he has had a drink from the little bottle Mother keeps in her apron pocket. The one that makes her cry.

I hear her shouting at him and then a loud crack. I know she is hurt, and her cries for help, "Please! Please! Please!" ricochet through my head. "No more. I don't want it anymore. Think of your daughter upstairs, she will be up in a minute and we don't want her to hear, do we?"

He does not care, my father; he carries on.

A knock at the door.

More shouting.

I think it is the man who lives in the house next to ours; he does not sound happy.

He shouts.

Father shouts.

Mother shouts.

They all shout and scream words that I do not know.

They are so angry.

The door slams.

I make my way down the stairs, as I am ready and dressed for school. I creep but know the stairs will squeak to let them know I am there. I hear hustle and bustle and the door slams! I venture into the kitchen and see Mother with her crying bottle in her hand and tears just glistening on her cheeks. Her eyes are so red that I know she has been there for a long time, crying and rubbing her eyes.

I run up to her and give her a big hug. I am sad now, too.

I have toast for breakfast. I eat and somehow I cannot swallow… I cough, but I feel the toast in my throat, I cannot swallow…

Oh goodness me, I begin to panic. I can't swallow... *Will I die...? Is this the "die" that mother talks about?* My dying? Now Mother is hitting me on my back; it hurts. I cough and cough and choke but it will not move. It is stuck. This is the dying; I know it is. I begin to panic more now; this is the dying.

Ouch, one more slap on the back, I cough and out it comes. Mother cries, again she cries and holds me so tight it hurts. This is not my dying. Not my time to die.

Grandmother takes me to school. I look up at her smiling face; I love her, and she makes me feel warm inside. She briefly speaks to my teacher about the toast episode this morning. Then she leaves to go home and I run to my friends, and we continue the day at school.

There are no major dramas in this year, just the usual Mum drinking from the crying bottle and father shouting and not being here.

■ ■ ■

Jan Mayfield

As You Grow- 7 Years

I want my friends to come to my house. I go to theirs, and they have a mother and father there all the time. They love each other, they must; they cuddle and their mothers do not have a crying bottle in their apron. They all sit and eat at the table, and they talk and hug without crying. I have seen no red-eyed crying in my friends' houses.

My mother says no friends can come in the house in case my dad comes home shouting. This brings back the memories I already have of the male voice shouting. I am not sure how I know this, but I remember hearing it all my life. Somehow I feel I may have been hit by my father. I hear the footsteps that feel like a swipe across the head. Oh why do I have a father like this?

My sister, where is my **sister**? She went away and no one speaks of her. Until now I can recall my mother and grandmother speaking about her, and then nothing. I decided that the whispers are about her. *Where is she?* I wonder. I know I have a sister, but where, I don't know.

In those few years, you can see how what is discussed in Pre-A is mirrored in life. Before the age of 8, Jasmine had lived through 8 of the experiences chosen, all of which will have an impact in the future and will lead to her needing to learn to trust.

Her father's attitude and behaviour towards her mother could lead to self-belief issues. Also, because she was not allowed friends at her house, it alienated her from friends and she will need to believe that she can live her life without worrying about dying. It has been suggested from an early age that she 'might' die.

The whole point of talking about Pre-A is to give you a picture of what you have asked for in your life, albeit without emotions. What is so very important is how you receive the experiences and how you move on from them.

The more we eliminate the past from our now or future thoughts, the more we will move on to the next experience.

■ ■ ■

Chapter 3

WHAT IS TRANCE?
A Temporary State With Suspension Of Personal Consciousness

∞ ∞ ∞

Dictionary Definition of Trance

Spiritualism. A temporary
state in which a medium, with suspension of personal consciousness,
is controlled by an Intelligence from without
and used as a means of communication, as from the dead.

Segregating My Thoughts From The Words Of The Spirits

There they go again, trying to get my attention. My world is so different. Wherever I go, I see spirits in all different forms. There may be a grandma spirit with someone in a coffee shop, or an uncle spirit watching over the person on the park bench. This all adds to a more hectic visionary life.

I have learned over the years to separate my brain. I have one side that are my thoughts, feelings and emotions. The area above the other side is where all the non-earthly information comes in. I cannot imagine how I would feel if it was all mixed up, but some work in this way.

A connection to trance work has always been strong. I even went on a course with a "famous" medium. I was already working beyond the way he was teaching but just hadn't realised it. There are no benchmarks in my life and I often forget that many people choose not to open up in this way.

The spirits know that I am open to most things they give me; I must be to be writing this! I always use my, what I call 'spirit brain', when working with them as I cannot allow my earthly thinking to interact.

■ ■ ■

How Do I Trance?

It all began with meditation, very slow short sessions and over the years I have learned to be able to take myself off into an altered state.

School lessons that were all very drab often led to a gaze or two out of the large panes of glass. To begin watching the rain as it bounced on and subsequently ran down the almost opaque screens of glass was mesmerising. Before you knew it, you were on a wonderful daydream and in the distance you could hear your name being whispered.

That was not a whisper...that was the teacher shouting your name in your ear but you were so far away in your daydream you could hardly hear it.

Trance can be best described as that daydream, and then a step or three deeper into the daydream. This is the place where the spirits will come and talk. Total relaxation to the point that you cannot feel the furniture you are sitting or lying on. As you go into the state, it is normal to see colours, pictures and people, most will have no relevance to where you are going. You are flicking though the channels!

Very rarely is there full memory of the tranced information. I allow this to happen and chose to be in this altered state and I know I can come out of it at any moment. Although sometimes it feels unearthly as I journey back up, so much so that I just want to stay a little longer because of the serenity.

My readings and private sessions are often conducted in an altered state but not as deep as the trance for the dialogues in this book. I can tune in and be as deep as I want to, whenever I want to.

The work for this book always had a rest day from trance to enable me to type up the recordings into dialogue format. The words that have been spoken are typed exactly as they come out of the recording. As I type the words, in my mind I am taken to that trance session and it all becomes a memory. Now, when I look and read the session, I am in that trance but awake as me with the feelings of the trance scenario.

The day or morning before a session I always ask the spirits if there is anything I need to know or do. Sometimes I may be told to place a crystal or stone somewhere, reposition the chair or simply they may want three instead of two candles lit. In the beginning, I would sit on a chair, always the same chair. This chair is for the purpose of this book, it is possible to trance anywhere.

One day the voices told me that I would be laying on the healing couch for the following session, I have this in a different room and only use it for healing. I added a few blankets, I was told to light a candle and put on some music prior to the session. This, I did and you will see in the book the point at which this happened.

For the purpose of *Zoetic Soul*, I was not to know who I would be trancing, except on one occasion when

I knew Grannie Mary would be there. I was only to say that Grannie Mary would be coming through to speak to Ques, which is the abbreviation I give to the person asking the questions. I was told not to say who she was as not to influence any line of questioning.

The recordings show how the depths of my breathing change from very slow and shallow to a rhythmic pant on other occasions. Sometimes in trance and in daily life when I have a connection coming in or when I want to go a little deeper, I always seem to exhale more than I inhale. I don't know the reason for this- just that it works for me. This can be heard on the recordings, and as I change from one voice to another I seem to exhale for longer. There has also been comments that I do this when I give readings, I exhale noticeably at the time of a deeper connection. This is just my way of working; I am unaware of this at the time.

As you read the Dialogue chapters you will see how the trance sessions are meant to be, with that wonderful connection to the voice of spirit.

■ ■ ■

Jan Mayfield

Chapter 4

'SUICIDE PASSINGS'

Secure

Understanding

In

Changing

Ideals

Death

Eternal Life

∞ ∞ ∞

Introduction To Suicide Passing

Six months prior to writing this, I was aware of increasing connections to those wanting to gain closure around loved ones who had taken their own lives. As a medium, I totally trust in spirits; they give me the information to relay to others.

Remember, I see death as the soul leaving the earthly body to be relocated back in the universe; returning home, some may say to paradise and others, heaven. In my eyes, it is the same place. Life is eternal.

Focusing on the souls who had taken their own lives, they all gave me information to validate their presence. More importantly, I was shown visions and given the ability to become that person's soul for the time of the reading. I tranced into the emotions, persona and the events leading up to their passing. The soul's account was and is so very different from how those on earth see it.

One example is as follows:

On a one to one reading with a lovely lady, I connected to a young male energy who had passed some years before. He had taken his own life, but no one knew how.

I acknowledged the spirit to show I was ready to channel his energy. Describing his personality was the point at which we began. She validated the tranced informational facts as accurate, to her knowledge.

I am now totally the male energy, I see through his eyes and have his feelings, and I will describe what I felt as him, what he told me to say.

I am walking up to a bridge, I am feeling really strong and I want to take on the world and win the battle. My body is encased in bright silver armour shining brightly as the sun reflects off and creates rainbows. I walk up the bridge and pause a little at the peak in the middle. Looking to the left over the railings I can see a river in front of me; a hill is to the left front. I feel so strong and happy, I am smiling and have that sort of knowing feeling that I am doing everything right and it is a good day. I am on top of the world.

I continue to walk down the other side of the bridge. I turn to the left at the bottom of the bridge and walk into the field of long clumped grasses gently waving in the breeze. As I walk forward, I look to the left and see the castle. Oh my, the castle is where I need to go; I look up to the turrets all square and protruding as if ready for action. I see the drawbridge is up and the river is the moat of the castle. The sky and the water are shades of clear azure blue.

As soon as I become parallel with the castle, I begin to walk towards the water in the moat. I look across and I see the castle as a very large building. I see the vastness, and within me I feel the strength and determination and the knowing that I need to be in that castle. My eyes are focused on the turrets where I see the flag flying in the breeze on this beautiful summer's day.

I step forward and with my inner strength and knowing, I walk into the water; I am the brave armoured soldier walking into the castle, ready for any battle that comes my way. As I walk forward, I do not reach the castle, I just walk straight into the river and let it engulf me.

Death by drowning.

What you, the reader, need to understand is in the eyes of the person taking their life, they are not unhappy. They saw no danger and were not alone. It was all so natural and what they wanted to do. This was their time to pass.

■ ■ ■

One morning I woke up and had the voices in my head (spirit voices- this is normal for me) telling me to go on social media and ask people for permission to connect to a loved one that had passed through suicide.

My Post Read..

"On a serious note. I am looking for people who have lost someone, who have taken their own life (suicide). This is research, confidential and I only want your permission and the first name of the person who passed... if you are interested please pm me or leave a comment and I will pm you... thank you. If you don't want me to know you on here, then mail me jansmail@!!!co.uk... thank you xx spiritual always xx"

The response was overwhelming. I remember thinking, ok so now I have over 100 names of people who have friends and relatives that have passed over due to taking their own life. What do I do with them? This is where trust and believing comes into play. I had to trust.

Periodically over a couple of years, I had seen a lady in the town where I do my writing, but did not know her. One thing led to another and we were talking about spiritual stuff. I did know at this point that I would trance the spirits of those who passed in this way. I also knew that I needed someone there with me. It is not something you can ask the average person to help you with. She was very good and open minded and was with me for the trance work.

We planned the time; it was to be at my place as the energies are right. Before we began, the voices told me to put a chair in the corner of the room and I was guided to place some crystals on it. Over the years I have used a small crystal pyramid in my healing sessions. Enhancing the energies in the room, the pyramid can be likened to any crystal but shaped into a pyramid. This was to be the chair that I sat on for the trance work and is now the cover of the book.

The trance sessions were recorded with the two of us in the room. The lady I met who I refer to as **Ques**, took a few notes as I spoke in trance; at the end of each session we discussed what happened and what was said.

The following day, I would listen to the recording and transcribe the dialogue as it was spoken. There is this raw sense of the different personalities that came through.

We began to work through the list asking for or asking who was with us, but the names never tallied and sometimes there was no name. I kept telling myself to trust and all will become clear. All the dialogue sessions were given a number which replaced any name given in the session.

I do feel that I, as me, am not here to think. I am guided and I allow guidance.

The following chapter is all about suicide and those that passed by taking their own life in this way.

You can read the dialogues on the following pages. I have trusted that spirit have given me this in the most sensitive way for those of you left on earth, who have knowledge of this type of passing. I see this work as a way of allowing you a glimpse through the window of suicide.

Abbreviations in the following section

JIT: - Jan speaking in trance

QUES: - The person asking the questions

JAN: - Jan as Jan

001-011 - The different souls talking through Jan

Jan Mayfield

Sessions 001-011

Transcribed dialogues of the recorded tranced sessions between 17th and 20th February 2015

001

002

005

006

007

008

009

010

011

You will notice that 003 and 004 are missing from the list. These two could not be transcribed as they did not record.

001

16-20-Feb-2015

Present in the room

JIT: Jan in trance

001: Jan as the spirit/soul voice

Ques: Asking the questions

JAN: Jan as Jan

Reference to home is the spirit world.

Jan makes herself comfortable and begins to take herself into her altered trance state for this connection to channel their voice.

Ques: Help me to understand your journey to going home, (leaving the earthly body) **001, were there Guides or someone waiting? Can you help me on this please?**

Pause

001: I was delivered back home, want to live back home.

Ques: Were there people there to help you?

001: There are always people to help.

001: I will show Jan, Jan can see. Just wait for one moment and I will show her.

Takes a long break here

001: They nearly did not like it when I called myself 001.

001: I was always created to go back; I knew when I would go. Life on earth is always complex, everything in my mind is complex.

001: Been to earth many times. People call me an old soul; they did not know what that meant to me.

Raises his voice here and seems a little agitated

001: Old soul meant to me that in my head I heard all the voices in my head.

001: All the time of all the souls that came before me, I did not let go when I came to earth, all the voices came with me. I did not leave them. First one, then another. Then another. Then another. Then another. Then another.

A bit louder and rhythmic

001: All the voices came into my head, men and women, children and pets' animals and dogs; all the voices and all the languages they were all in my head.

001: It was alright to start with then they came, my head filled with the voices all trying to show me the way, their way not my way.

I let them talk, they didn't really listen, but I let them talk.

Statement

001: I lost my legs, I cannot feel my legs. My right arm too.

001: I have this feeling of whiskers *(whispers)*

001: So, the journey began. When I listened to their voices I turned my head from side to side to hear the different voices. Sometimes they made me jump so I would turn my head quickly, like flicking my hair. I hear the voices. So my journey began.

Pause, then quieter voice

001: I tried school; they said I did not listen, but I listened to the voices in my head, *pause* no-one can hear them. I could see. I could see through my eyes they were like pools of water everything seemed to ripple concave. My eyes were concave. When I looked out at the people they looked at me and they looked at all the people's voices not just me. I like voices. I like horses. Hooray Henry! Can you tell? Can you see all my voices?

Can you see all my friends in my head? No. I like talking to myself.

Pause

Ques: Why did you choose this way to go, 001?

001: I did not choose. It was the voices. They needed me to be one of them. I didn't choose, the voices told me and I listened. Is that choosing?

Is listening choosing? *More of a statement than a question*

Ques: I can't answer that 001, only you can answer that.

001: They show me; they showed me home.

I like home.

Ques: Can you help me understand the process you went through?

001: The process?

Ques: Was it a process, 001?

001: No.

Ques: Did you just know?

001: Yes of course.

Ques: How can I help the people left behind understand what happened?

001: The people left *(pause)* will never understand as they don't hear the voices.

001: If I come back to earth without the voices, I am not 001. Only people with the voices are 001. People without the voices will never understand, people without the voices will blame, and people with the voices will interfere.

001: People without the voices will think they know what is going on in your head. Because they don't have the voices...They only think. They do not hear the voices.

Ques: Can you stop the voices, 001?

001: I cannot stop the voices.

001: People without the voices will blame themselves. People without the voices try and help, people without the voices will think. People without the voices will...

001: I cannot stop the voices; the voices were a malfunction when I entered the womb.

A long pause here now

001: When I entered the womb the voices should have stayed at home they did not go; they came with me. The voices I carried. No, I did not carry they are there in my head all the time.

Hehehe, he is sounding very cheeky and mischievous

001: Sometimes I like it. Sometimes I look at people and see lips moving and do not know what they are saying. I just hear the voices.

001: One day my voice said, *(whispers)* *let's go home*. Then another one said, *let's go home,* and another one said *let's go home.*

Such a soft whisper

001: All the voices then said *let's go home, let's go home, let's go home, let's go home*

Ques: What did they ask you to do 001?

001: Let's go home, let's go home *(whisper)*

001: They wanted me to go to sleep. They wanted me to go; to leave my earthly body. They wanted my beautiful soul to rise, my soul did rise. From that day my soul did rise from that body, my voices were with me but different. I can see the voices now all different colours beautiful, beautiful.

001: Beautiful spheres of knowing, we speak without words and transfer energy. We are all the same- all my voices and myself- we are all the same.

Ques: Are you happy there, 001?

001: Happy, is an earthly emotion. I don't need earthly emotion. I am in the most beautiful precious place. I am home. I am still learning. I am still learning to grow. I look and see people who used to look in my eyes and speak. I look at them. They are not happy.

Ques: Have you done this before 001? How many times have you done this before?

001: Done what before?

Ques: Come down and the voices have told you to go back?

001: Just one time, just one time I had a malfunction.

Ques: Do you need to come again and repeat this process?

001: No! I passed. I passed everything that I came to do. Why would I come back?

001: Why?

001: My life is complete on earth.

Ques: Are there any words that I can say to express to the people that you left behind? Are there any words? A knowing that I can pass on to them to ease their pain?

001: For them to know however hard they tried to help me they could not help me. The voices in my head helped me; I was unique.

001: You have your life on earth. Each individual person you have your life on earth. Understand this, totally understand this; you have your life on earth.

001: You could not help or change or make it easier or harder. There is nothing you could have done to change what I was feeling, what I was seeing, what I was hearing- you could not change it. You must realise that people who go back with the voices generally have a malfunction at birth or before birth.

001: This is what they are meant to experience. Now I am home I can see that everything I experienced was what I asked for. I wanted to experience all those things. You see I am happy to have experienced it... *(thoughtful)* It is only your perception of my voices that made it feel uncomfortable; your perception of me did not feel right. But my perception of my voices... *(pause)* was not always uncomfortable and it was meant to be this way for me.

001: Live your life on earth and do not try and change the paths of others; help along the way and become friends but do not try and change the path of someone else.

Ques: Where are you now 001? I know you say home, but where is home?

Slowly and thoughtfully, said in the spirit voice

001: I am home in paradise. I am home and just a slight vibration away from you and an even closer vibration to the one you call Jan. Everybody wants to come and see, to come and sit with her and talk. She understands. She will show the people many things.

Just a vibration away, you will not understand if you think of houses and roads and hospitals and people and tables and chairs and vehicles and distance you will not understand. Think vibration and just a slight vibration away.

Ques: Are you at home and at peace now, 001?

001: Yes.

Ques: Is there anything else you need to tell me or that you want to tell me?

001: I want to thank you for allowing me a voice to help others in the future in the earthly body. Of course things are not how you may perceive them to be. I want you all to work together to make peace. I see the most amazing colours. Right now I see the bird of paradise flower as you name it; the beauty and symmetry all follow the point, it will always point in the right direction.

Breathes and takes a little break

Ques: Is it time to let you go now, 001?

Smiling and, quite upbeat

001: I have to say about the chocolate. There is chocolate, there is a beautiful smell of chocolate around I think this is for my family on earth.

Thinking, likes to remember the memories

I give them the beautiful smell of melting chocolate have no worry have no fear that I am home.

Changes voice a little, he wants you to see, a part of his world

001: I am learning you know. I sit in the library- not like your library. I can just look at a book and remember it. To the people you called the family of me, I have to say... the mole is dark; the mole needs to be corrected. The feet on the child turn in.

Louder and brighter now

001: The wedding will not go without a hitch!

Breathes

001: I have to leave now.

Ques: Thank you 001, thank you for your light, thank you for your time and thank you for your wisdom.

001: Thank you too.

JAN:

As I began to come out of the trance I felt like I was paralysed, sensing his arm and legs had problems. Initially, I could not move mine.

Clearly he was not released of all his past lives as he came to earth; the voices were his past lives.

When I was him at home I felt warm, special, connected and loved. I was enveloped in this beautiful velvet fabric that felt so lush. As I reverted to him on earth, I felt cold, empty and unloved but I did not feel unloved as earthly terms but as 001 I felt unloved with the voices.

A beautiful innate sense of love, happiness and warmth was felt as I transcribed.

■ ■ ■

002

16-20-Feb-2015

Present in the room

JIT: Jan in trance

001: Jan as the spirit/soul voice

Ques: Asking the questions

JAN: Jan as Jan

Jan makes herself comfortable and begins to take herself into her altered trance state for this connection to channel their voice.

Before actually connecting to 002, I had an overwhelming, beautiful sense of a very warm energy.

Ques: I want you to help us understand the journey you took to going home to where you are now.

Ques: Are you happy to do that? Would you like to tell me?

Replied with a very positive

002: Yes.

Quizzically said

002: What do you want then?

Ques: Did the guides come to you, 002?

Ques: Why did you want to go home?

002: It was my time to go home; it was my time.

Ques: Did anyone tell you to do this?

Ques: Did you choose to do this?

002: I am happy to go- was my saving grace you know.

Ques: Why was it your saving grace?

002: Before I did not go.

Ques: Did you do it before, 002?

002: Do what?

Ques: Try to go home before?

002: Yes.

Ques: Did it work?

002: No.

002: I knew it was right.

Ques: Did someone stop you the first time?

Breathes deeper

002: Intervention.

Ques: Who intervened?

002: People in white coats *(he laughed)* I am happy now. But I am happy now.

Ques: Did they try and label you with a condition?

002: They gave me tablets.

Ques: What did the tablets do?

002: They made me sleep.

Pause

002: I want to pause for a moment.

Ques: Ok 002

Long pause softly said, thoughtfully

002: It's very calm inside, I like to be on my own, I like to feel peaceful, I like to feel happy. I like to be alone.

002: Why did you want me to be with other people, why did you want to take me out of my happy? Why?

Ques: Who wanted to take you out of your happy, 002?

Whispers

002: Everybody.

002: It's not good for you, 002 it is not good for you 002, but I am happy.

002: I am happy, I was happy. People in white coats, people wanted me not to be happy. I want to sit in my garden. I like to be peaceful. I like to see faces as they came out of the sky. I see faces, and the clouds were there too.

Smiling as he spoke

002: Did you do that?

Ques: No I like to look at the sky, not clouds.

002: Did you not see the faces?

Ques: No, I didn't see the faces.

002: I did.

Ques: Did you hear voices or just faces?

Ques: What did the people in white coats say to you?

Slowly speaking

002: They said it is unnatural. To see the clouds. To see the faces. To be on my own for so many hours, in a day, in a week, it is unnatural.

Ques: How can I explain this to your family you left behind, 002?

The word MIND is emphasised in a loud, determined voice

002: To them to say 'my world', to say that this was a happy place for me. I needed quiet. I needed peace.

002: This word depression that was not me inside. I was at peace and happy reminiscing in my mind, thinking in my **mind**, my life was in my **mind**.

002: I might not move and I might not be animated but my world was in my **mind**.

002: I came to earth to experience my mind, not running, not physical, not partying, not laughing, not this, not that. I came to experience my **mind**.

002: You said I shouldn't. You said I can't. You said it is not natural.

002: My dear people on earth, I was in the right place.

002: My mouth became sore.

Ques: Why is your mouth sore, 002?

002: I can't remember... *Thinking*

...I think I vomited.

I think a tube went inside.

Ques: How did you choose to go home, 002, can I ask you that?

002: I did not choose.

Ques: Was it an accident to go home?

002: Nooo.

002: It was for me to take my **mind** back home. I saw the angels as I lay on the bed with the white coats. I saw the angels. The angel that has the trumpet.

Ques: Was that Gabriel?

002: Yes! Archangel Gabriel. I saw Gabriel as I lay on the bed with the white coats. I saw Gabriel above me. I reached up to Gabriel - you pulled me back.

Ques: Was it your time to go with Gabriel?

002: You pulled me back.

Ques: I did not pull you back, 002

002: The white coats.

Ques: What were the white coats doing to you, 002?

002: I don't know. I wanted to go.

Ques: Is that why you didn't go home the first time?

002: You pulled me back you made me stay. You tied me down, not literally. When I woke up I felt awful.

Ques: How did you go home the second time, 002?

Jan breathes deeply and a long pause

Quietly spoken

002: I don't know but I didn't like to be back. It was not for me to be back as you would say. I wanted to go home.

002: My face never felt right, my left side and my face.

Hears people talking

002: Everyone came to look at me. I can hear them... *so glad you are here, we want this, we want that, what would I do without you...? Breathes a sigh*

That's better.

Ques: Did that make you sad, 002?

002: Yes, very.

Ques: Are you at peace and happy where you are now?

002: Yes.

Ques: Have you got anything to say to the people you left behind?

002: That I love the new baby. I adore and love the new baby. I watch over the baby. I am the guardian angel for the baby. I watch over the baby.

Ques: Is that your baby, 002?

002: No.

Ques: Whose baby was that?

002: Tis the baby now.

Breathes a sigh

Loud and meaningful, laughs

002: Well where that caravan is now then, things have changed.

002: One day when I wasn't allowed to be in my peaceful mind for so long. I so longed to be in my peaceful life.

002: I was like someone who could do anything... anything I wanted I could do in my mind. So one day in my mind, I was a cowboy I made a lasso, I lassoed the cattle.

I could almost feel him smiling, he was so happy

002: Very happy. So much fun, shouting to all the other cowboys on a ranch, a bit agitated sometimes.

He now becomes agitated in his voice

002: Doing this and doing that. Moving here and moving there.

Ques: Where were you most at peace on earth, 002?

002: In my mind. One day I lassoed cattle. It felt so wonderful. One day I lassoed a tree.

Ques: Hmm, you lassoed a tree instead of a cow?

Quiet, serious now

002: No my lasso got caught in the branches.

Serious and stern

002: In my mind I can climb the tree. 'Cos I can do anything. Remember I feel so free. Remember in my mind I can do anything. I feel so free.

002: I climbed the tree.

002: In my mind I am free.

I can feel such a sense of, well-being and trepidation here

002: Ecstatic in my head and mind feeling invincible, feeling amazing. I am feeling wonderful I climbed the tree. I slid along the branch and dropped into the branches.

002: Ahhhh and then I was home.

Ques: Is there anything else you want to tell me?

002: Yesss...

Paused

002: Nothing hurt. Nothing was bad. Did you see Gabriel?

He whistled, 002 whistled here, whoo whoo, getting louder towards the end... he laughed.

Very upbeat and happy here

002: I liked it that Gabriel came and whisked my soul back home hmmm hmmmm.

Ques: Are you whole and complete now, 002?

002: I am home as a spherical being.
At peace and where I should be. Everyone only visits the earthly body.

Ques: It was a burden to you wasn't it, 002?

002: NO!

Ques: You liked being in the human body?

002: Yes!

002: I liked living in my **mind,** liked climbing the tree. I liked seeing the people. I liked being a cowboy. I liked... Everything was as it should be. Why does everyone try and change it? Why did they hold me back on earth, why?

Ques: So if you liked being on earth and the people in the white coats were not happy with you, in your mind you knew you had to go home?

002: Yes.

Very informative and stern

002: When you enter that birth canal or the womb you have already asked to be there so many years; it is prearranged.

Ques: So was there a malfunction when you came through?

002: Malfunction?

002: No!

002: Why would I have malfunction?

Ques: I was just curious

002: No.

Ques: Have you been here before, will you come back again or will you stay with Gabriel?

002: I shall return but not as 002. I shall return.

Ques: Do you know who as yet or not?

002: It's not my time. No I have things to do at home first, before I visit that place I have things to do.

002: Remember earth is the learning ground. I have things to do here now.

Ques: When the time is right you will pop back here?

002: I like to have experiences.

Ques: So have you been before, 002?

Ques: Have you been here before as someone else?

002: Yes.

Ques: Who were you before?

Ques: Am I asking too many questions, 002?

A feeling of agitation as the questions are too fast

002: I need a moment.

002: Too fast.

Ques: Ok, I will slow down

There is a pause now, I felt like he was recalling past information

002: In the dark I was getting the coal. In the dark I was getting the coal and the shaft broke. 23 people died that day. 23 people went back home.

23 people, I was one.

Ques: What were you called then?

002: Arthur. (name change)

Long pause here

I feel a searching

002: The busy streets... the busy streets was another. Bicycle bells.

I sit, I sit on the edge.

Ques: Are you still 002?

002: No, I sit on the edge. I am hungry. I have the bells. I smell the spices. I see the colours- so many people.

Ques: Who are you now?

002: Not 002.

002: Mohammad. (name change)

002: They shout, Mohammad! They shout, Mohammad come and help me! I smile and laugh. I felt wanted as they call my name.

002: Ah you won't recognise the words.

002: 6 years I feel...

002: Mohammad

002: 6 years, I am 6 years. Everyone loves Mohammad.

Long pause, he is thinking

002: Ooo Mohammad

002: Mohammad had to go back home too.

Ques: How old was Mohammad when he had to go back home?

Answered fast

002: Earthly years of 11.

Ques: How old was Arthur when he had to go back home?

002: Earthly years of 23.

Ques: How old was 002 when he needed to go back home?

002: 47.

Ques: 002, am I speaking to 002 now?

002: Yes.

Ques: Do you just come back when you need to learn something?

002: Of course, my dear.

Ques: I think you are a very wise soul, don't you?

002: Yes of course.

002: I have access to all things great. I have access to everything. I am everything. I am a Supreme Being. Why would I not be? I am home.

Ques: Will you come back soon?

002: No.

Becomes more animated now

002: Tell them the headaches need to go away. That earthly woman cannot live with the headaches. Right hand side of her nose and over to the back of the neck.

Ques: Who is that, your wife?

002: No just that earthly woman, she will know. Tell her to get rid of the headaches.

Ques: Is there anything else I need to tell anyone down here for you?

002: To remember the toasting fork...

Each 'remember' is said with emphasis and meaning

002: To remember the coal fire

002: To remember the diamond

002: To remember the monogrammed handkerchief.

Ques: Was that a present from you?

002: No.

002: To remember the silk.

002: To remember the church blessing.

002: To be guided to hear me. Don't pretend you can't hear me when I speak- you can listen, listen to me. I will show you the way.

002: Who drove the wrong way down the street? Who gave toffee to the person that made their teeth stick together?

Laughs

Loitering speech

002: I have no wish or desire to visit yet but I will help the people I left behind. The people who still have lessons to learn, I will help.

Ques: Have you got anymore to tell me or have you done?

002: Done?

Ques: Is there anything else you want to tell me?

002: I like it. I like it.

Ques: What do you like, 002?

He says with a lovely satisfied feeling

002: Home.

Out of the blue he goes on to say

002: I see pigs.

Ques: Pigs?

002: Pigs on earth.

Ques: Who are the pigs on earth?

It makes me smile here as I recall the feeling when he said this

002: Pigs. Pink pigs

Rests, voice changes

002: Just give me a moment.

Much more meaningful now after the pause

002: Healing is needed. Healing is being sent, did you know?

Ques: Did I know what, 002?

002: Remember I told you about the clouds?

Ques: Yes.

Slow, meaningful speech

002: I am telling you now inside the clouds is the most amazing beautiful purple energy that rains down. Those that stand in the rain will be healed and cleansed to enable them to move forward in their earthly life.

You can speak to Jan now.

Ques: Thank you 002, it has been a pleasure meeting you.

Ques: Have you gone now?

JAN:

Yes, he has gone… I am still in trance but not speaking as an energy that has passed.

I am shown a couple of images. I see a market town, a school desk with an ink-well and something to do with a teacher.

There is a moustache which I feel maybe a joke within the family.

A lighthouse with love for everyone and Canada too.

There were two characters here; one clearly had a mental illness who was likely to have been sectioned and took tablets which made him feel happy.

There wasn't a malfunction. All was as it was supposed to be. Which begs the question: Are some of us born this way? Is this part of our journey? Is this Pre-A?

Mohammad had to go home early, he was loved by everyone. He indicated that life for him was very poor.

As I type, I can recall the wonderful sense of love that resonated with Mohammad. The freedom and beauty as 002 passed became emotionally overwhelming. Thank you.

■ ■ ■

005

16-20-Feb-2015

Present in the room

JIT: Jan in trance

005: Jan as the spirit/soul voice

Ques: Asking the questions

Jan: Jan as Jan

Jan makes herself comfortable and begins to take herself into her altered trance state for this connection to channel their voice.

Before connecting to 005 Jan had a feeling of being ashamed and shy, and she wasn't sure if he wanted to speak.

Ques: Hi 005.

005: Hi.

Ques: Thank you for coming through. Is it ok if I ask you some questions?

A pause

005: Yes.

Ques: Can you tell me about your passing, please?

005: No.

Ques: No?

Ques: Is there anything you would like to tell me rather than me asking questions?

005: Give me a moment.

JIT: This person feels very sad and lonely

I feel pain and discomfort in my eyes

Long pause

Long pause

005: It started at school.

Ques: What started at school, 005?

The following was said in a robotic way

005: Jacket was too big, they took it off me and ripped it. Put it on the floor and made a circle around me. They started singing and shouting, kicking and pointing at me.

005: Jumped on my coat, onto the floor.. jumped on it. Walked away and laughed.

Ques: How old were you when this happened, 005?

005: Don't know, maybe 11.

Maybe before

Maybe before...

Ques: Is that why you passed the way you did, 005?

Very quietly spoken

005: Yes.

005: I used to go and sit in my bedroom.

005: Inside I used to feel sick. I just feel sick, I wanted to vomit.

Ques: Did anyone help you, 005?

005: They used to tell me to eat it up and I'd feel better. I put it in my pocket. Phew why did I sit there? I had to stop going to that table and sat in my bedroom. Bring it on a plate throw it away...

JIT: I could see 005 putting his food in his pocket because he did not want to eat it

Ques: Could anyone help you, 005?

So very quietly spoken here

005: Not yet.

He remembers

005: But they just keep looking at me. I can see a face looking, the lady used to keep looking at me even crying. She cried, she cried...

Ques: Is this your mother, 005?

Hmm he thinks

Very quietly spoken

005: Late.

His voice is back to a normal range but faster and more pronounced

Pause

005: Don't think I have been here long you know.

Pause

Ques: Do you think it was your time to come, 005?

005: Bit confused really, shall I go or shall I stay?

005: When I close my eyes, I see things.

Ques: Is there anything I can help you with 005?

005: Just a moment.

005: I close my eyes. I see things. I lay on the bed. I felt sick. It is very quiet. I just let it all happen. I did not fight back. I could not fight back.

Rhythmically spoken

005: Something in me told me not to eat, not to eat, not to eat. I was hungry. I felt sick…

They told me not to eat… not to eat, not to eat.

Big pause

Ques: Is this how you passed 005, not eating?

005: Stop it then.

005: No one believed me. Mum said I would be alright tomorrow. My grandma died. My grandma got taken, my grandma went.

Such sadness in his voice as he remembered

005: Where did my grandma go? Love my grandma. She was there I love her. Phew.

Breathes a sigh, exhales

005: She made me feel sick, she is not there now.

005: Love my grandma, she used to tickle my face, stroke my face to make me go to sleep. I smile as I recall.

005: I wanted to be with Grandma again. All the time I wanted to be with Grandma.

005: I went in to the place and spoke to a man. I did not want to speak. He spoke to me.

005: The man thought he was helping me.

005: But I wanted to go to Grandma.

005: Feel sick.

Raises his voice

005: Don't eat that food! Don't eat that food!

Slow pause, low voice

005: Tired now, tired.

Pause

005: Tired - go to Grandma.

Ques: Do you want us to find your grandma, 005?

A long pause here, Jan feels the internal pain of grandma

005: I am with Grandma now.

Ques: Good.

Peps up here and a lot brighter

005: Fire...

Fire burning.

005: They said I would go to hell. Miss the fire burning. To see the fire burning.

005: What do they know, what do they know?

005: With grandma now.

005: There is no hell, who said hell?

Ques: How did you pass 005?

005: Beautiful sleep is what I remember, what I can tell you is beautiful sleep.

Pause then out of nowhere

005: My throat hurts.

More pauses, I feel he is deep in thought

005: I didn't shout; I went to sleep.

Thank you.

Ques: Was it your time to go, 005?

Meaningfully said

005: My grandma was calling me.

Long pause

Ques: Is grandma happy you are together?

005: Yes, we sit and talk about earthly life. We meet up and chat together. Then we do what we need to do.

Ques: Is this the first time you have been here or have you been here before?

005: First time I come in an earthly body, for a short time on earth I stay.

His voice changes now to be more determined

005: I am waiting around now.

005: Scientific exploration is what is needed.

Long pause

Ques: Did you learn your lesson this time, is that why the people were horrible at school, 005?

005: I learnt my lessons. I am with my soul family now. Next time I come to earth, I will be wise beyond my years. I will be the one who shows the way.

He is excited as he speaks

005: I will be an **INVENTOR**.

005: Scientific knowledge with equations. My journey to earth will be calculated.

Ques: When will you come, 005?

005: I don't know.

I feel he thinks about earth now

005: Scotch mist is what they say, scotch mist.

005: Adding to that earthly family. Poor were the people on earth blaming, self-destructing self. Pep up yourself.

005: I lived my time on earth.

I sense a smile

I am happy now to be with Grandma.

Ques: Is there anything anyone could have done, anything to stop your passing, 005?

Firmly spoken

005: No.

Ques: Is there anything you want to say to your family on earth?

005: I needed to break free from the cotton wool you say you wrapped me up in.

I needed to break free.

(He is telling you that all was as it should be, no one could have done anything.)

005: My journey, my path was only short. I could not break free you see.

005: From the acorn grows the tree. Plant more acorns make more trees.

He is very clear now

005: Listen, believe what you hear, not what you think might be there.

Pause

005: Amazing oranges, purples and turquoise. I see. I see before me the light dragon energy. Fires over the people, the earthly family, the dragon energy is all around.

005: God is within you all; do not ask God the questions. God, does not question God. For doing that you question yourself. God is inside, God is you and understand this and you will see that my life on earth was meant. Carry the load and yours will be short. You see small people; small people walking up a hill symbolically carrying the loads of everyone else. Let go of your load and slide down and continue across the way. You need not to walk the tight rope; the path is wide for you.

The whole mood changes now and he quickly recites the following

005: Show me the Hillman Imp.

005: Show me the leather seats.

005: Show me the magician who can't perfect his tricks.

005: Show me the checked slippers.

005: Show me the sewing machine that seems to work alone.

005: Show me the 19th July.

005: Show me.

Ques: What is significant about 19th July, 005?

He says sternly

005: They will know.

005: Show me the rubbish bin that overflows.

005: Show me the pantry.

005: Show me the money, show me Christ. Show me.

005: Show me puddings and show me beans.

005: Show the garden with the swing.

005: Show me.

He stops there and pauses for a while

005: Grandma is calling now.

Ques: Is there anything else I can do for you, 005?

It is like he forgot to say a couple of things

005: I want to tell the man about the Peanuts cartoon.

005: I am going now. On the newspaper.

Ques: Bye, love you.

005: I hug you. I hug you.

Ques: Me or Jan?

005: The voice I hug.

Ques: Thank you, I hug you back with love and light.

JAN:

This was a very strong character who was obviously bullied at school and wrapped in cotton wool by his family. This led to him not being able to break free from those constraints. (Maybe he could if he had wanted to.) He would not be himself, he too had voices that told him about the food, which seemed to have led to an eating disorder.

He talks about God and wants people to know that to question God is to question one's self. Are we all one?

To be united with his grandma made him happy, as her passing made him so sad in an earthly emotion.

We are beginning to see a large separation between earthly and home perspectives.

As I typed and reflected, there was this wonderful sense of knowing, knowing that all is and will be fine. I felt the oneness too, the oneness with self.

■ ■ ■

006

16-20-Feb-2015

Present in the room

JIT: Jan in trance

006: Jan as the spirit/soul voice

Ques: Asking the questions

JAN: Jan as Jan

Reference to home is the spirit world.

Jan makes herself comfortable and begins to take herself into her altered trance state for this connection to channel their voice.

JIT: I felt that this soul was far away; at one point I wondered if he/she would come forward. Once the connection was stronger there was a feeling of urgency.

006: I am here now.

Ques: 006?

006: Yes.

Ques: Hi, 006?

006: Hello.

Ques: Is it ok to ask questions or do you just want to tell me?

006: You can ask questions.

Ques: How did you go home?

006: I swimmed.

Sighs

006: I want to show you everything. Everything I want to show you.

Ques: What is important?

006: You tell me what is important to you.

Ques: What can you show us to help us understand?

006: Emptiness.

Breathes deeply

006: I am empty of that within; I have the brain drain that empties all within.

Ques: Did you choose to come through like this, 006?

006: It is my learning; I have the brain drain. I have the brain and the drain, then I want to do it all fast, then they say what do I know, then I see it upside down, they say what do I know.

Mixed up

006: Why do they show it to me like this?

006: Upside down turn around, why do they show it like this?

006: Inside out upside down. I can't see it the same as you.

006: Ha.

A bit of a pause here and continues to speak at speed

006: They give me the blue one, they give me the white one, little tiny circles of hard crystallised things to make me feel better.

Ques: Tablets?

006: They didn't make me feel better.

Ques: Now?

006: I still see; I still have the brain drain. I have the brain drain.

006: Envelopes passed from one to another I see on the desk with the man behind, pen in hand looking and wondering what will he say. What will he say every week I visit the man, what will he say?

Almost singing now

006: The brain drain, the brain drain, the brain drain…

Hahahahha he laughs

006: Navy, navy blue come and sit next to me, no you go alone, no come and sit next to me.. no you go alone.

I'll stay here no come with me.. No I'll stay here, no come with me.

Big sighs and slowly says

006: The brain drain.

Ques: How old are you, 006?

006: 15.

Ques: Is there anything anyone could have done to help you on this earth?

006: Yes.

Ques: What could they have done to help you?

He rhythmically speaks of the brain drain

006: Plugged the brain drain. Plugged the brain drain, plugged the brain drain. Look it is going out, it all comes out it is only there for a little while then it all comes out that's what you say. It all comes out. It's lost. It all comes out. I know it is there but the door is closed.

006: The door is closed to that bit inside. They closed the door.

Ques: Is that a malfunction?

006: No.

Ques: Is this a lesson you needed to learn?

006: Lesson? A path, my path.

006: With one door closed before I come to earth, I am a strong educated business man. I know I have one door closed.

Ques: How many times have you been on earth before?

Thinks

006: Many hundreds. Many hundreds of times but they never closed the door before.

Pause, long pause

Indicating there is more than one door

006: They asked me how I know, of course I know. That door is not closed, that door is closed, and that door is closed.

Ques: Did you choose to go this time, 006?

Deep breaths

Pause

Ques: Or was it an accident?

006: It was always meant to be; short lived they say door closed, they say short lived.

006: Back home is special. I like home I could visit home in my mind as I lay on my bed. I could visit home.

I could sit in the chair. I would visit home. All the times I visited home.

Ques: Did they give you a label on earth, the people that gave you the blue and the yellow?

006: I have a green one now.

Ques: What is green, 006?

006: To put in my mouth tablet.

It feels like he wants to release those thoughts

006: Cheshire.

Ques: Did they give you a name when you had to take the green tablet?

006: They closed the other door... Depression and recluse.

006: I'd see the panda before me. I would see the Queen of Hearts. I would see the diamonds in disguise. I would see far beyond earth. I would see another pill they gave. Another door they close. I'd take myself up home because they closed too many doors.

006: I am sad now, all my doors are closing. Too many doors now.

Ques: Are you at peace now, 006?

006: Yes.

006: Goodbye.

Ques: Goodbye 006, take care.

006: Thank you.

Ques: Love and light.

006: I will show Jan now, some more...

Pause

Long pause, rather quickly spoken

JIT: I can see beautiful kites flying.

JIT: I can see amazing reflective shades of purple.

JIT: I can see healing that needs to be done on earth.

JIT: I can see the troubled with voices and visions and past paths that had been closed.

JIT: I see Rowntree.

JIT: I see squirrels.

JIT: I see the breathing changes I feel the shallow breath. I feel the breathing is restricted, gulps.

JIT: Give love on earth to everyone. I leave behind dear love on earth; 'tis my way to be taken. I did sit and wait a little in a place where I could have returned but I chose to carry on my journey home. To be with grandma.

JIT: Fish, shellfish.

JIT: I see the sadness and the black clothes. Why are you so sad? You let myself go. Why are you so sad? Go live your life. The one in the pram is all grown up, long life is there for you, never hide always show the true being you are meant to be.

JIT: Got some beautiful blue flowers being given to the people left on earth.

JAN:

006 faded quickly and I felt he didn't want to talk too much. He watched his own funeral and had the message to live your life as you are meant to do. His mind was very mixed up and knew that he didn't have the brain that others had. His brain was worse when he took the tablets. There was this sense of sadness throughout his life but not at passing or being home. Maybe the tablets numbed the outside but exaggerated the inside?

He gave me the insights for further snippets of information. I felt privileged to see the things he gave me and as I type this I have a great sense of achievement, somehow.

■ ■ ■

007

16-20-Feb-2015

Present in the room

JIT: Jan in trance

007: Jan as the spirit/soul voice

Ques: Asking the questions

JAN: Jan as Jan

Reference to home is the spirit world.

Jan makes herself comfortable and begins to take herself into her altered trance state for this connection to channel their voice.

JIT: Sensing a sense of shyness, an insecure energy coming through.

Ques: Hi 007.

Replied with a very low voice

007: Hello.

Ques: Are you ok for me to ask questions?

Ques: How old were you when you passed?

007 was very quiet, and very slow as he spoke; it felt like he had his head down and was looking to the floor

Slowly the words came

007: 43.

Ques: Why did you choose to go this way?

007: It was my time.

Ques: Sorry, can you say that again please?

007: It was my time to go.

A pause

He continued

007: I like football and a bit of rugby now and again I can see them playing crazy golf, candy floss.

Chirped up here, his voice was quick and meaningful

007: Happy days.

He is smiling now

007: She screws her face up only when she is thinking, or thinking about me, she screws her face up.

Statement from no where

007: I like working with Jan.

Ques: Are you happy to be working with me too?

007: Yes.

Ques: Is there anything anyone could have done to change the path you took?

007: No one.

Takes a breath or two

007: Tea and biscuits always make you feel better they say.

Ques: Can I ask you how you passed, 007?

007: I was happy to go.

Ques: What led up to you going, 007?

Ques: What led up to the week or month before?

007: Just a moment.

The question was too quick

Very quiet now, he took time to think; we waited for him at this point I could see lots of purple and white

007: I am quite sleepy.

007: I am tired.

Ques: Why are you tired?

007: I don't know, just tired…

His voice fades with lots of breathing and sighing

Slowly spoke

007: Well things were not right. Things felt different. Things took a turn. I cried you know I cried in the toilet. I used to go into the bathroom and sit on the toilet and cry.

Sounds incredibly sad speaking very slowly; inside I feel sad too

Ques: What was making you sad 007, why did you cry?

007: My head.

Ques: Sorry?

Ques did not hear what he said; he has a quiet muffled voice

007: My head.

Ques: What was in your head?

007: Sadness and tears. Failure. Not being good enough, wanting different, wanting more, no one saw what I could see. What I could see.

Ques: Did you not tell anyone?

007: I tried.

A quick sentence follows. I think he wanted to change the subject

007: A jackdaw in the garden.

007: Nice neat flowers I wanted to kick them.

007: I am not a violent person.

007: Closed it away and held it inside.

Ques: You bottled everything up?

007: Inside.

007: I think I had an illness before.

Ques: What illness?

007: I don't know...

007: I started thinking about the happy-land, the homeland, going back home.

Ques: Have you been here before, 007?

007: On earth?

Ques: Yes.

007: Many times.

Long pauses

Speaks in a slow voice

007: The spirit in the personality has gone. I feel so drab. I feel boring. I have no vision. It's empty. I look forward to what?

007: Because I am empty, I go on empty.

Ques: Is this called depression?

In a very low voice

007: They say.

A pause now, and then

007: You are never totally alone in this world. there is always someone there to help you.

007: The earthly world is full of people wanting to help you. Why don't they leave you alone and let you go to where you want to be?

Ques: Is that why you chose to go, because it was your time?

Ques: So no one could have helped you or stopped you from going?

007: No.

Deep sighs

Ques: How can you explain to the people you left behind that all was ok?

007: Because it was my path and my journey, my decisions. It was ok because it was my decision. It was ok because it was my decision. They chose for it not to be their decision. They have different paths in different ways. They are blinded by their own visions and think that everyone should share their visions…

…It is my vision and my vision only

Space to think, quiet

Ques: Are you at peace now?

Very strong words, very meaningful voice

007: I am very happy now and always, always thinking knowing, always being able to do everything, always transferring my energy by thought I am at one and peace. And at peace now I am home.

Ques: Will you come again?

007: I am in the beautiful purple orb field; I live in the purple orb field.

007's voice has changed; it is very strong and to the point, making statements

007: Someone had poorly teeth on earth. They will need to have their wisdom teeth pulled.

Very strong rhythmic speaking here

007: I am in a beautiful purple energy looking down and around the earthly place that I left behind.

007: I look down and see, I look down and see. As I look down and watch you as you come out of your doors and into your vehicles drive along you should walk more…

Still very rhythmic

007: You should walk more till your heart pumps till it misses a beat. You should be in the fresh air.

007: You should be in nature.

007: You should be breathing in the divine energy looking for the different vibrations, so you can be at one. Being calm and at peace with yourself, will take you to the place you need to be.

007 then spoke in a very confident, knowing way the word:

007: Home.

A pause is taken here

Ques: What else do we need to know, 007?

His voice has changed again, very strong and almost sounds deeper.

007: Interconnecting Galactical airspace.

007: I meet the people from the planets never seen by humans. We jump from one to the other and I see the vibrations as they shift, a little here and a little there. My time on earth is done I now shall be…

Pause

007: Galactical.

Deep breaths, resting

Ques: Is there anything you want to say to those left on earth?

The following few paragraphs flow very easily, methodically and in a meaningful tone

007: Keep your beautiful memories and smile at the thoughts that come into your head. Know that I am around you; my energy surpasses all thoughts that you may have. My energy surrounds you at all times. I am at one with you. Just give me a gentle thought and I will be there.

007: Everything is not as you imagine it to be. I cannot however, I cannot explain to you because you as the earthlings do not have the vision that I see and want to portray to you.

007: You are closed minds.

007: This is how you are meant to be for your journey to earth, but I cannot help you. You need to know that I am well and happy. You need to know I am where I am supposed to be and everything is as it is supposed to be.

Continued in a very positive way, giving us a statement

007: The earth will close, the earth will darken, and the earth will brighten again for the future. Tend to the earth and make things right. Tend to the earth and grow the right things. Tend to the earth and you will be rich, rich from the earth you will be.

There was a pause and all of a sudden in a strong voice

007: Galactious expedius.

007: Galactious atrancious.

Galactious, maiden voyage the maiden voyage for me is near.

Big pause, I felt like he had gone but knew he was still there

Ques: Are you coming back to earth plane, 007?

A categorical

007: No!

007: Galactical I will be.

007: I speak this I tell you. Galactical I will be. I speak the words.

007: You know we learn all the lessons on earth at that time. Then we pursue different planets and areas for more testing times but none as hard as earth.

Ques: How many times have you been to earth?

007: Many thousands, I cannot count.

Pause

007: Why count?

Big pause

Deep and meaningful

007: My light shines bright. My light shines bright for the future.

He continues quickly

007: I have a few words to the people on earth that they think I left behind.

007: Let me go. Relieve me from your thoughts, continue with your path, live each day as if it was your last; be happy. Use all the tools that you have in your mind even if you are not sure where they came from. Use all the tools you have in your mind to move forward in the most peaceful and enigmatic way. Bring forth the stars that shine above, allow them to shine within you. Move forward my dear little earthlings, move forward on your path.

Be bright as a daisy.

007: Look out for the university that has the course for the child to develop, look out.

Whistles

Straight in with these words

007: March, March I give you the march. I give you the month of March I give you the month of March many changes come in March embrace the changes.

007: You will need a parachute in June take the parachute for a happy landing.

007: I see champagne in July drink the champagne but not too much!

007: How does your garden grow?

007: The restaurant with the brown table and chairs the brown window frames the smoked glass. Chic.

007: I see you go.

Tuneful

007: *Mmm hmmm hmmmm.*

007: Stratford-upon-Avon I see you visit looking up at the houses. I'll be on the roof watching you. You just look I will be the shadow that passes by.

007: Give you Scotland for a magical time.

007: The brays of the north ring true in your ears, the brays of the north ring true.

007: I see horses galloping, galloping like there is no stopping them, galloping like the wind. Follow the horses at your pace and gallop.

007: Shine the shoes dear one keep shining the shoes. Maisie is the name. Blessings.

JAN:

This was the last thing 007 said. He left. I had the feeling that he had said all he wanted to on this occasion.

He gave the impression that he is excited by the prospect of his future and wants those left on earth to continue in their lives, knowing that is what he is doing. You too should create that sense of excitement for the magical mysteries of earthly life to unfold.

■ ■ ■

008

16-20-Feb-2015

Present in the room

JIT: Jan in trance

008:   Jan as the spirit/soul voice

Ques: Asking the questions

JAN: Jan as Jan

Reference to home is the spirit world.

Jan makes herself comfortable and begins to take herself into her altered trance state for this connection to channel their voice.

JIT: I had an urgency inside me; he wanted to come and share this information. I felt very grounded and knew everything felt right.

Ques: Hi 008.

Deep and distant was the response

008: Alright.

Ques: How old were you when you went home?

Like it did not matter

008: I don't know, really.

Ques: Do you want me to ask you questions or do you want me to listen to what you have to say?

008: I will speak.

There is a pause

Ques: What do I need to know, 008?

008: Silver paper.

Shouts towards the end of the following sentence

008: I tried the silver paper, OK! I tried it!

Makes short statements

008: There was a baby…

008: It was all mixed up…

008: I tried the silver paper…

008: Then there was a baby…

008: I tried the silver paper…

The momentum and volume increases

008: There was a baby… I tried the silver paper…There was a baby.

008: Let me open up to the light, let me become one with the light; let me open up to the light.

He whispers

008: I see the light.

008: I see the light before me. I try and walk towards, I just can't get there.

Ques: Are you not in the light?

008: Yessssss.

008: Before.

Breathes deeply, sighing

008: It's cold now.

008: Can't stop can't stop s st st stop shaking.

Shivers and stutters

Ques: Without the silver paper?

008: Yes. *Oh god goodooohhhhhh*

Ques: Was it an accident, 008?

008: I need the paper first, light the matches. Light the paper!

Relieved

008: Ohhhh ohhhhh thank you.

008: Ohhh ooohhhhh makes my head feel good, my head feels dizzy.

The feeling was of sarcasm, mocking someone shouting his name.

008: 008! 008! 008! 008!

008: Where is 008, what is he doing, haha! I smoke the silver paper now.

008: I see the baby too; I want to reach out to the baby.

008: The silver paper calls me back. I love the silver paper; it glistens and shines.

JIT: Looking through my eyes as I am shown the silver; it is very bright and glistens. It feels so welcoming. He is happy to see it but there is not a desperation.

008: I hear that baby cry. I want to go to the baby.

008: The silver paper calls me, all bright and twinkly. Hmmmmm the silver paper calls me.

Ques: Did anyone try and stop you, 008?

Replied in a quick and meaningful manner

008: I did.

008: I stopped the paper.

008: I stopped the silver paper.

008: I saw the baby. I held the baby.

008: I loved the baby. I stopped the silver paper.

Pause

Ques: How?

Quickly holding his head, he went on to say

008: I have the evil inside. I had the evil. It would not go.

008: Inside my head I saw the faces... they would not go... closed my eyes. I saw the faces.

Repeated methodical pattern

008: I drink water. I sweat. I drink water. I sweat. I drink water.

Ques: Is that when you were stopping the silver paper?

008: Give me the silver paper. Give me the silver paper.

008: No no.

Ques: Was it an accident?

008: Too much silver paper for me hmmm.

Deep breaths here

Ques: Was it your time to go?

008: Yes, my time was there, I take the silver paper.

008: Once, twice, three times.

This is very low whisper

Pause

008: Happy inside.

008: The little beauty all around.

Slowly says

008: I see the uniform that stands beside me.

Pause

008: I see the crazy lives flashing all around.

008: I see the baby and the people on earth, as I rise above.

Pause and now meaningfully goes on to say

008: Gorgeous gems are there for you, take yours and live your life. Rainbows and diamonds shining on the wall. Live your life my child I will be the guardian one, my child I will look after you.

008: Look after you.

Breathes deeply as if remembering

Ques: Is that your baby, 008?

008: Love the baby.

The tone changes to lively and upbeat

008: Who is going on TV?

Ques: I don't know 008, who is going on TV?

008: Well they are talking about TV. Well I can do this and you can do that. I hear them say.

008: I see frogs leaping about. I see long-tongued lizards and chameleons ahh.

He continues speaking rather fast

008: In the glass box they have them. I show them I am there. I switch the lights on and I switch the lights off. I show them I am there. With the lizards and chameleons in the cage.. I show them I am there.

A pause

008: Bring me the light, give me the light, show me the way forward. Give me the light, give me the light. Show me the way forward.

Mmmm

008: Show me the way now.

008: You will never understand. I cannot tell you how to understand. You will never believe. You will always blame, that is your path to follow the blame of your minD.

Big emphasis on the letter D

008: I am happy now. I am at peace. I follow my child. I grow with the child. I am the guardian of the child.

008: Red buses I see the London. In the family as I watch you go to the place to the lands you have never seen before I watch you go.

Street lights are new as they shine down on the property that will be for you. Look out for the street light I say.

008: Look out for the 3 and the 8 on the door. The one that will give you the one, the new life will be at 38.

A little pause here

008: Dismiss the forked-tongue words from the one who tries to show you the way.

Dismiss the forked-tongued words I say.

New breath

008: You are given guidance from above. Take it. Silence your mind and you may hear.

Pause

Quieter now

008: Silence your mind and I will show you how to live the earthly life to fulfilment. Your life is long. Two females, I see and the child. I see your life is long.

008: Live them, feel them, be them, breathe them, taste them, drink them.

008: Your lives are long.

Breathes deeply

Waits

Now fast and loud with an almost smile on his face

008: See that brown Typhoo monkey.

008: I see the bolts and screws that hold things together.

008: Know that I am at peace and at one with my life.

Quieter now

008: Know that my life was meant.

008: I see the foot one foot larger than the other.

008: I see the clogs that someone wears.

008: Follow your heart dear, follow your heart.

008: Ravenstone is the word I give. Makers of plastic.

008: The daytime hobby that turns to a business. Make the money from your hobby.

Great delight as I see you smile at the newcomer into your sight.

Thoughtful

008: Great delight.

Long pause

Soft and distantly, spoken in a meaningful way

008: I am going to leave you now and continue in my beautiful homeland.

I am a red sphere and I did meet my twin flame on earth.

Very slowly and quietly as though he was walking away

008: Blessings…

JAN:

Out of all the dialogues I have transcribes and proofed, this one always makes me cry. You can feel the love for his family and the awful addiction that he never quite came to terms with. As with all of the passings, there is a repeated sense that everything is made up of light and happiness in the homeland.

■ ■ ■

009

16-20-Feb-2015

Present in the room

JIT: Jan in trance

009: Jan as the spirit/soul voice

Ques: Asking the questions

JAN: Jan as Jan

Reference to home is the spirit world.

Jan makes herself comfortable and begins to take herself into her altered trance state for this connection to channel their voice.

This connection was a little disjointed at the beginning.

009: Play the music. Play that music.

009: Feel dirty.

Ques: Why do you feel dirty? Who are you?

009: I don't know, feel dirty and feel bad.

A sadness with a feeling of being lost

Ques: Why?

Does not know why, confused

009: They won't play the music.

Ques: Why does music make you feel clean?

009: I like the music in my head brain, dirty no music.

Ques: What's dirty?

009: Dirty inside head, please let the music play. I don't want to listen.

Ques: Listen to what?

He becomes slightly agitated

009: To them.

Ques: Who's them?

Pause

Ques: Who's them? Who's them?

Just a moment, he becomes more agitated

Ques was asking too much too quick for him, he needed time to think

009: *Them* are the ones that interfere; *them* are the ones I hide from. *Them* are the ones I move from.

He speaks as though he does not want them to hear

Ques: Where are them?

009: All around. Earth ones. *Them* are here, *them* are there, *them* are everywhere.

009: Play the music, they go.

Ques: What is the solution?

009: Solution is to keep playing the music, solution is let me hear what I want to hear, solution is to not interfere.

009: Rock and roll is here to stay.

(Music seems to be a therapy for him.)

009: Doctors... did not want him to listen to the music. It was wrong.

009: Why can't earthlings understand?

009: Leave me alone, live your life not mine. Life without the music is sad...

Life without the music is always short. Life without the music

He pauses and thinks, sadness

009: He was such a nice boy. He got taken too soon. Too soon.

009: I came to do, I came to see, I came to be, I did it! I did it!

009: Lived my life I went back home.

009: I don't understand questions.

Ques: What questions?

009: Earth family questions; I live life shown to me and I go back home. Interference is no good, I chose it.

009: You try and change... What's...

Pauses, I feel deep sadness

009: I see water from your eyes.

009: If they let me do what I want to do then you will understand this and not have the grief.

009: They have to live their life; evolution is forever evolving. You cannot save the people contracted to come for a short time.

009: Do not take on the conditioning start now and show them.

009: Cultures do this; we take a bit from each religion there is only religion.

Ques: What religion?

009: There is not religion we are one, we are collective. Begin now and do not take on conditioning. It's not difficult begin now...

Ques: One step at a time?

009: No! Great strides, leap forward, strengthen and telepathy, strengthening telepathy. Encourage them to think their thoughts, encourage them to. Open brain will see that moving forward is the key.

009: Solidarity music, let the music play.

009: Use the brain that you don't use... This is the key, to use this brain...

Ques: Who are you?

009: 009.

009: I am 009. That is all you need to know.

009: Earthling called Jan I will show her more, she knows.

009: I am going now.

JAN:

Everything was quiet and still, he had said all he needed to, but I had a sense of more to come later.

There is a clear message here, to live our lives and to know that we are and will fulfil our life's purpose if we listen to our inner guide. He was a strong character as he delivered his messages to us. I had no sense of the homeland as I typed, only messages for earthlings. With a sense of achievement.

■ ■ ■

010

16-20-Feb-2015

Present in the room

JIT: Jan in trance

010: Jan as the spirit/soul voice

Ques: Asking the questions

JAN: Jan as Jan

Jan makes herself comfortable and begins to take herself into her altered trance state for this connection to channel their voice.

Reference to home is the spirit world.

010: Ahhh.

High energy

010: If I had a pound in my pocket for every time I said that.

Ques: What, 010?

010: It's 010.

A pause here

Ques: How old are you, 010?

010: 52.

Ques: How did you get home?

Thinks, pauses

I feel bouncy and energetic

010: Haven't you got enough now?

Ques: Enough what, 010?

010: Why do you want to know?

Ques: Because we need to understand 010, it is hard being on this earthly plane when you don't understand.

010: It's always, it's always events, different events lead up to it, and it's always…

010: My mum died, my mum went to heaven.

Ques: Did you choose to go or was it something that just happened?

010: It stopped.

Ques: What stopped?

Touches chest

010: Her heart.

010: It's only the vehicle.

Ques: What, the body is only the vehicle?

Ques: You understand we need to move on.

010: I don't know why they have sent me to talk to you.

Ques: Why?

010: Well, what can I tell you?

Ques: You can tell us what happened, 010.

010: You don't remember all that stuff, what do you want me to look at that now for?

010: When I came home they made me look at it.

Ques: What did they make you see, 010?

010: I had to sit there, with the chief, I call him the chief. It's not him or her but I call him the chief.

010: *Hmm*

He is smiling here and quite jovial

010: Chief Silver Toes.

Ques: Chief Silver Toes?

Smiles

Laughing

Ques: I like you, 010.

Ques: What did he make you do then, 010?

010: Well he made me watch it all on telly, didn't he?

Ques: What, how you got here?

010: Oh yes, it wasn't really a telly but you know it as a telly.

He swings off on a tangent remembering…

010: We used to like watching the horses you know, watching them racing around.

Hahahha

Ques: Bit of a gambler were you, 010?

010: No not me, keep me pound in my pocket.

He is a character

Laughter

Ques: Bet you had a few pounds in your pocket after watching the horses?

010: Oh yes.

010: They never really understood me, you know?

Ques: Who?

010: Them people.

Ques: What, the people up there or the people on earth?

010: People on earth, they all understand me up there.

Ques: Bit of a character were you, 010?

010: Weeelll I was on a mission like.

Ques: What was your mission then?

010: To survive.

Ques: What were you trying to survive?

He smiled

010: The end DATE.

Ques: Did you not want that date or did you choose it yourself?

010: I chose it.

Ques: Did you choose that particular date for a reason?

He changes the subject

010: Lots of purple. I can see lots of purple coming around me now.

Ques: What's the significance of purple?

010: It is such a beautiful colour; a spiritual colour. I will say it like that so you will understand me.

Ques: I am interested to know what you watched on that TV 010, old Silver Toes?

010 talks so fast, like it does not want to recognise but recalls for Jan

010: Well mmmmm from birth to end everything… bomb-bomb-bomb- bomb-bomb, and then they stop it and they say well if you had of done this and done that you would not have done this, non-nom-nom-nom then they show you something else.

Such speed he is talking

010: *You would have done this and you would have done that ner-ner nern-ner* and I was saying, *well, I couldn't do this and I couldn't do that.* And they didn't show me this, but… Then they rewound it and showed me something else. If you had picked that 2 bob up off the floor and gone into the bookies and had a bet on that horse that I was thinking about. Something to do with the peacock then I would have won loads of money and I wouldn't have been poor and kept my money in my pocket.

Phew, this was all said so quickly without taking many breaths

Ques: Yes, but would you still have gone the way you went?

010: Yes.

Ques: Ah.

Ques: So did you choose to take yourself rather than your mum with the old ticker stopping?

010: Not a choice- I decided, I decided that is what I wanted to do. I knew it was going to happen. I could feel it inside me when people talked about the suicide I knew that is what I would do, I could hear it. I could hear it, I could hear it. Sometimes my mind got jumbled up, so jumbled up.

010: I didn't know whether I was coming or going, upside down or down side up and my brain was jumbled, it didn't really matter.

010: Everybody liked me.

Ques: You sound a right character.

010: Good.

Ques: So could anyone have done anything to stop you committing suicide?

Ques: Did Silver Toes like the fact that you had done that and was he a bit annoyed that you had gone that way?

Agitated with the fast questioning

010: You are asking too quickly.

010: Why would he be annoyed?

Ques: Well because you said to me he showed you all these different choices.

010: Yes, this was not a choice. It was in my plan.

Ques: Ahhh.

Ques: Ok, ok I get it now.

010: The choices are, what can I say, how can I tell you, the choices are the choices are...

He is thinking

010: The choices are...

010: Like I chose not to pick the money up, I chose not to see the money. Therefore, I didn't make any more money. That was a choice.

Ques: Ah so you chose to go this way?

010: If you like.

Changes the subject as he feels Ques does not understand

010: I got very tired you know.

Ques: What were you tired of?

Ques: Life?

Got the impression he did not like to have words put in his mouth

He gave the impression he did not like the questions

010: No just tired. My body made me tired, everything went- all my energy. All my hair, all my everything.

Ques: Did you have cancer, 010?

010: I think that is what they called it. My hair came back it grew again.

Hahah it grew spikey.

Ques: Hahha a bit like a punk rocker?

010: Yeah.

010: Do you remember them?

Ques: Yes, I used to like them, old Sid Vicious

010: Yes.

010: But it grew back and I was still tired. I was still tired, *oh he looks alright now doesn't he,* and *he looks alright he is on the mend*. They did not know what is going on inside.

010: Just a minute now.

A long pause he is thinking

010: Don't ask me any questions.

Ques: I will wait for you, 010.

After a long pause he is ready to speak again

010: She wants to get her hair done, see the goat, what about that toffee she made; hard as rock it was.

Ques: Can I ask who made the toffee?

010: No.

010: Used to hear her crying.

Pauses

010: Something about clowns, the clowns and crying they had their fingers cut off too.

It all feels very sad here

010: Well, I could hear her crying. This one came and that one came and I knew, I knew from before how I was going. I just knew and I knew it was getting close.

010: They all said I looked well. They weren't inside me were they? *Come inside me* I used to think...

He pondered his thoughts

He mocked...

Almost singing the words

010: Yes, yes I do look well. I look fine huh.

As he remembers

His voice is stronger now and more powerful

010: Penultimate. Penultimate.

010: Hum Mars Bar in the fridge. Oh Mars Bars.

010: Connection.

010: Rugby.

010: Marseille, Marseille. Oooo laaa larrrr.

A little laughter in his voice as he smiles at the memories

010: Moulin Rouge...

010: We send her healing you know. We can do that. We send healing to people, earthlings, you know we can do, I send it down now.

Quite a pause here

010: Big toe and gout.

010: The little one around now in the orchard and apple trees, before she used to pick them up and make a pie.

010: So you see my dear, it was the illness the happy faces saying I looked alright that led to my departure. I departed in a peaceful way- no pain or aches, I just departed. They all looked on and cried, ashen looking faces. It was ok. I knew I had to go.

010: No feelings, no emotion, just looking, not even wanting to stay to make it right. I knew I had to go. You see it was my time.

Hmmmmm

010: It's good here you know; it is good. We can do anything we want to do, remember we are not an earthling we can do anything, anything. Anything.

Ques: Even watch the horses?

He laughs a little

010: Could pop down to Aintree if I wanted and scare the favourite.

010: I don't know. I have learned things that I have not had time to do on earth.

Big pause here

010: I learned to disconnect bombs.

Ques: Bombs?

010: Mmmm I think they are bombs. I learned to be precise and calculated in my movements.

010: We are all different you know. There are green ones, orange ones... *he thinks*

Ques: Silver feet?

010: He does not see us very much he watches over; he does not sit with us.

010: We all sit together in our colours when we have been to earth and are HOME again. If we have been enough times, we change colour and become a different colour and that is how we are.

010: Earth, Earth, Earth. *(Like 1 2 3)* Back different colour, different colour and we just keep building up like that helping the young ones.

Ques: What colour are you now, 010?

010: I am orange.

Ques: How many times have you been back 010, to be orange?

010: 1000s. We don't really keep count. I just said it like that for you. Still learning, it's what we achieve and how we live the earthly life more times.

Ques: So are you going to come back again?

010: Four more times.

Ques: Will you get silver feet?

010: NO, many things to do before silver feet. **Ques: If you come back 4 more times, what colour will you be when you go back after the 4th time?**

010: Pardon?

Ques: If you come back 4 more times, what colour will you be when you go back after the 4th time?

010: Red.

Ques: Can I ask you a question, 010?

010: Yes.

Ques: How do you get your colours 010? What colour do you start at?

010: You start pale...

Ques: Yes, then what colour?

010: Like, hmm, not really a colour, like a shade, hue, not really a colour. Start pale iridescent beautiful sheen. Just move along, move along, move along.

Ques: So what comes after pale then, iridescent?

010: Opaque.

Lots of thinking here, like his mind is somewhere else

There are too many questions that are meaningless to him

Ques: And after opaque?

010: Ooo you don't want to know all of them now. There is too many, I got a black one then.

Ques: What is black for then?

010: Black is authority, but not how you know it.

Ques: Ok then.

He is thinking whether to tell us or not

Long pause

010: Black is for Galacticus.

Ques: What is Galacticus?

010: Moving between the planets and moving between the stars, we do that as well you know.

Ques: Believe it or not Galacticus on earth is a TV programme.

010: And what do they do?

Ques: They just go off in a space ship and have adventures.

010: The same then, we don't have adventures, we learn.

010: Everybody wants to finish earth and be Galacticus; it is time. We have time, time is infinitum. We have time, there is no time. It just is. Jan sees it.

010: That one you call Jan, she watches. She comes through I see her; she comes and has a look and goes back.

A short pause... as if to say that is enough of that for now

Loudly says

010: Right, what else then?

010: Do we go now?

Ques: Do you want to go now?

Ques: I don't know do you want to go, or is there anything else you want to tell me?

010: No more now.

Ques: It has been lovely meeting you, 010.

010: HP sauce.

Ques: Nice on chips...

Very quietly said

010: Bacon.

Ques: Are you leaving us now, 010?

010: Thank you.

JAN: He leaves, he is gone...

JAN:

I had a beautiful feeling of a family man; he is very proud to be where he is now. He became very irritated with some of the questions. I sensed he thought they were irrelevant, and I feel on reflection that there could have been some in depth investigation with the questioning. Especially as he was the first one to mention about watching his life on the TV screen after he passed over. Missed opportunities which may be answered later.

He was a little shy at first and didn't seem to grasp why we wanted him to talk about his earthly events. I felt a northern accent with this one, who was not settled in the spirit world- homeland.

■ ■ ■

011

16-20-Feb-2015

Present in the room

JIT: Jan in trance

011:   Jan as the spirit/soul voice

Ques: Asking the questions

JAN: Jan as Jan

Jan makes herself comfortable and begins to take herself into her altered state for this connection to channel their voice.

Reference to home is the spirit world.

011: Sigh.

Ques: How old are you, 011?

011: I am not sure. I don't know.

Ques: Do you think you are young or older?

011: Not old.

011: *Hmmmm.*

Ques: What do you want to tell me 011, or do you want to ask me questions?

011: Well nice of you to come here, what do you want to know?

Ques: I want to know lots of things, 011.

Ques: I'd like to know how you got home.

011: I flew.

Ques: Wow, why did you choose to fly home?

011: The angels.

Ques: And what did you do to make the angels come?

Long pause

011: I did that, is it electric?

Ques: Was it a heart attack, electric paddles?

011: Yes, I saw the angels and then they did that and the angels went.

Hmmm.

Ques: But they came back for you?

Ques: What did you do to make them do the paddles on you?

Long pauses

He seems to be distant

011: It was in the car.

Ques: Were you driving?

011: No, no one.

Ques: What were you doing in the car?

011: The garage...

Breathes deeply

011: It smelt so good and felt so warm... hmmmmm...

He really liked it

Ques: What made you sit in the car and get that nice smell?

011: It smells - lovely because...

Long pause

011: Because.

Pause

011: They did this to me.

Ques: Who did that to you?

011: People.

Ques: Why did people do that to you?

011: I knew they were there.

Ques: The Angels?

*011 becomes very **agitated** with the rapid questions*

011: No. Might have been God.

Ques: What happened a month before you sat in the car, 011?

011: My life was very busy with people always asking me things, people not knowing things, people asking me things.

He seems a bit confused here

011: This one, that one, my head...

Ques: Was it just too much pressure, 011?

Ignores the question

011: Then I could hear the voices.

Ques: What voices were they?

011: The voices of love.

Pause

011: The voices loved me and made me feel good. Every night they cuddle me and tell me it was good. Told me to do things. Told me to go out the house in the middle of the night and go for a walk; when I came back everyone shouted at me.

011: I went for a walk for 3 days. When I came back, the police were there saying I had gone missing. I had only gone walking with my friends. They told me to go.

Feeling of sadness and confusion as though he doesn't understand

011: So I didn't go walking anymore.

Ques: Were your friends in your head?

He asks quizzically

011: In my head?

Ques: Yes, the friends you went walking with?

011: They talked in my head and walked in front, they turned around making sure I was there and holding out their hands to guide me to go the right way. There was a big black hole but I was not to go in it, so I carried on walking.

011: They showed me different things, they showed me a rope, they showed me tablets, they gave me a knife and a gun they showed me all different things and had to choose which one I wanted.

Ques: Which one did you choose?

He thinks for a minute

011: Tablets. I took the tablets.

Long pauses

He remembers

He is mixed up and hallucinating

011: I had to walk. The Mermaid told me, *later you will feel better if you lay down.*

Very calm slow speaking

011: I lay down closed my eyes, so beautiful, so peaceful.

Exhales deeply

011: It was not my time. I see the angels and lotus flower.. know where I was going, feel my self-going...

Very loud

011: WhhaaooooBanggggggg!

Ques: Made me jump then!

011: Maize Maize...

Very loud again

011: WhhaaooooBanggggggg!

011: Where are my angels?

011: Where are my friends? Now I can see them in the distance, are they coming back?

011: Ooooooo going haaaaaa, I am going, turn around and have a look.

011: Look at the watch. (*He shows me someone looking at their watch as he looks back.*)

011: Hmm, I am gone now.

He feels very calm

011: Help me along, I open the door number 4 in we go... whoooaa

I see very bright lights

011: The lights are bright orange, white, yellow, spectrum colours.

He tells himself to…

011: Walk forward. Sorry. Walk forward.

011: Oooomm that is nice. Some familiar faces. They are a bit blurred but I can see who they are so I keep walking with the angels. A lion as well.

011: It is a long road, a long path here we go a bit like…

He thinks of an earthly term

011: The yellow brick road.

011: Hahah

Long pause here

011: Like.

011: One day I came back; I don't like coming to earth. One day I came back to help someone.

011: I am turquoise.

Ques: What is the significance of turquoise?

011: Well you know… I *urm* I have special,

Ponders

011: I have different; I have… How do I explain to earthlings?

011: Different.

011: I come to earth and stand beside...

Pause

Ponders again

011: I can change the course; one day I came to earth because I could see someone driving. I could see a motorway and someone driving along it and I knew they were going to crash. It, I knew it was wrong, I knew it was not their time.

011: So I came down to earth, and I just moved the car a little bit that way. I moved that one a little bit that way, and the car I was helping just carried on through the middle. That is called divine intervention.

011: We can do that sometimes, circumstances led to it being the wrong time in the wrong place and it did not need to happen.

Ques: Are you a guardian angel then?

011: Not exactly not for one I am the...

Hmmmmm thinks of the word

011: I don't know how to explain for you, not a guardian angel.

Ques: An overseer?

011: Like an overseer, I look and I get warnings. I get told when something like that is going to happen. I just have a little visit to earth and make changes and then I go back again.

Ques: You are like a tweaker?

He does not understand

011: Tweaker?

011: I did it for Jan. I tweaked for Jan. She sees me now.

Breathes deeply

Said quickly and abruptly

011: Questions for me now because it is time to return, please.

Ques: Not sure what I need to ask you if I am honest, 011.

Ques: Is there anything you need to say to the people you left on earth?

011: Just to know that everything is right. Everything is going forward as it should do and that if I feel your journey is wrong, I will be there to help you. Make sure you put your keys in your pocket, don't leave them in the door.

Pause

011: I am always around you sending love; feel the love, feel my love around you.

011: Hmmm, cloaking you in your life. Julie and Vanessa I see somewhere around that family, Julie and Vanessa.

Ques: Is there anything else I need to know, 011?

011: Sending eternal love and guidance to everyone God bless.

JAN:

011 is very meaningful and to the point, I have the impression that he is an old soul and has special privileges or their equivalent. He seemed to find it difficult to communicate in earthly terms but gave us a clear account of his life and passing.

I sensed more missed opportunities with the questioning. Although at some point we began with a set of questions, the tranced souls went off on a tangent and the questions were not used. As I was in trance and unable to hear what was asked, I was unable to intervene. This soul left me feeling accomplished.

■ ■ ■

I will not draw any major conclusions from the dialogues. I want you to find the points that resonate with your life.

If you have lost a loved one to a "suicide" passing, I know you have learned to accept the happiness of that person as they are home now.

Working closely with so many on earth who have lost loved ones and friends in this way, there is always a resounding feeling of happiness from the soul. Ready to go, it was their time; they are often more confused as to why earthlings cannot understand.

Speaking from a personal view, I see "suicide" as an illness that is no different to a heart attack or any other illness that takes someone home. Letting go of the stigma can release some of the guilt that is often there. It is something that happens, and takes people back home.

I will expand on this statement that 011 made.

"011: I did it for Jan, I tweaked for Jan she sees me now."

One particular day I was not feeling well, I could not function. My mind was all over the place and could not seem to bring my thoughts together. I knew that it was not right so I visited the GP, my usual one was off that day. I was given an appointment with someone else, he knew nothing of my history and listened to what I had to say, but didn't really look at me. He was typing notes as I spoke, he gave the odd grunt here and there to indicate he was listening.

He wrote a prescription for some tablets and told me to take them and I would feel fine. I like to use a more holistic approach to health but in this case I knew I needed help there and then. I took one of the tablets the following morning.

Soon after I felt a little light headed and my mind was still all over the place. I was commuting to my work base in Adult Education. The journey was approximately a 45-minute drive from my home. I would listen to the music on the radio and this seemed to cut the journey time in half as my mind was otherwise occupied.

That day, I drove in silence, because there was so much going on in my mind. I needed to release some of the thoughts but they would not come out. I remember driving along, I remember my foot on the accelerator and I remember the speed. I needed to go faster as my mind thought this would improve my thinking. I drove faster. It felt good.

I could see the street light coming towards me, the tall concrete leg that it stood on was looking at me. I needed to get to it. I was at a 45-degree angle in the middle of a Dual carriage way heading towards the street light.

I do not know what happened next, it felt like my car was being pushed; I remember taking my hands off the steering wheel and the car was miraculously in the right direction. I had hit the grass verge but not the street light.

This is what 011 is taking about, so maybe it was him who helped me not to go home that day. Did he tweak my car by steering me on to the road again?

I threw the tablets away.

That evening I was working in the local college and in the staff room, where everyone congregated before class time. I spoke out about what had happened. I did this because on the way to the college I was frightened as I was having thoughts of going on to the roof and jumping off. Those thoughts went after about 5 minutes though.

The response I had from the teachers in there was:

Don't be so silly, why are you thinking like that? Don't let me hear you say that again... I needed a hug.

The following day I saw my own GP and never took any tablets like that again.

I was saved because it was not my time to go home. I believe.

■ ■ ■

Chapter 5

TRANCING DEEPER INTO THE UNIVERSAL ENERGIES

∞ ∞ ∞

Jan Mayfield

Trancing Deeper Into The Universal Energies With The Following Dialogues

Issiah
Guilt Mirror
270215
5456
Black cat
Black Dot
Pretty Maids

Reaching a deeper level of trance for this set of dialogues proved to be an amazing experience.

As I tranced deeper, beyond thoughts and beyond meditation, my mind was taken into the universe to meet with the Orbs. Orbs are the way I see the passed souls in their universal habitat for this work. I see spheres of varying shades of colour and transparency. I am in this state of deep trance to be their voice. Communication is often through thought, telepathy and a knowing.

We have moved on from the suicide passings to be given this insight into life after/before earth and how our actions can bring about different pathways.

The names given in this chapter have no connection to the original list.

As you read the transcribed dialogue, imagine the space that I talk about as in the picture below, and imagine the rooms instead of the chair. Or use your own imagination and have your vision of the universal space.

Abbreviations in this chapter

JIT:	Jan in trance
ISSIAH:	Jan as the spirit/soul voice
GoldO:	Jan as the Gold Orb
Soul:	Jan as the baby soul
MAN:	Jan as the man
EarthO:	Jan as Earth Orbie, ones that return to earth
?:	A different person speaking
QUES:	Asking the questions

Issiah

23-Feb-2015

Present in the room

JIT: Jan in trance

ISSIAH: Jan as the spirit/soul voice

GoldO: Jan as Gold Orb

Ques: Asking the questions

Reference to home is the spirit world.

Jan makes herself comfortable and begins to take herself into her altered trance state for this connection to channel their voice.

JIT: As I enter the trance for this session through closed eyes I see that the whole of my space is lit up with a beautiful bright white light; to the left I can see turquoise swirls dancing as it enters my sight path. I have a strong tickle on my head which I know is from the spirits. They are very close.

Long pause

Thinking

Can hear whispers and then the voice begins

ISSIAH: Of course there are times when you wonder why. Of course there are times when you wonder why.

Pause

Retrieves historical information

ISSIAH: Show the people there was a point in history, there was a point before. Hmmm… there was a point.

ISSIAH: Never mind, we will carry on forward, forward we go, and forward we go. Through the ages I see thee. Champions of each era, I see the champions, I see the sword. I see the chariots, I see the gold and I feel the armour over my shoulders; I feel my helmet pointing up to the sky all cold. Chariots of gold, I see the cobbled roads.

Hmmmm

ISSIAH: We will have our place. We all have our time; we all have our Orbies. On earth we all have our strengths and weaknesses and how the strengths outweigh the weaknesses. Let the weaknesses fade and use your strengths to push you forward, work together as a team and look inside each other's minds. Work together as a team and look inside the minds of everyone.

ISSIAH: What happened? You let it all go wrong, didn't you?

ISSIAH: Precision and timings, building monuments, creating underground space to be protected, creating amazing beauty here on earth.

Ques: Who created the amazing beauty here on earth?

ISSIAH: Generations before it went wrong.

Ques: Why did it go wrong?

ISSIAH: Human interaction connecting technology allowed it to be. But never mind because we move along, we move along and we will see. Open the doors for you now. There you go.

Breathes, exhales

Ques: Did you open the doors now?

Talks almost rhythmically

ISSIAH: I am getting off the chariot and I am taking her to the door. I have to leave her at the door. I will take her to the door; there you go. Thank you.

Ques: Who are you taking to the door?

ISSIAH: Jan.

Breathes down deeper into trance

ISSIAH: Hmmm possession and possessed, possession and possessed.

Ques: Who is possessed?

ISSIAH: The earth is possessed with demonic traits. We cleared it once, we will clear it again.

ISSIAH: Just go through the door, go through the door, go and look, go on.

Ushers Jan through the door

Ques: Do you want Jan to go through the door?

ISSIAH: Yes.

Pause and low voice

Talks to self quietly

ISSIAH: Go on Jan, go on Jan.

Ques: What will she see through the door?

ISSIAH: I don't know. Give her the door, the door is a gift. Open the door, open the door.

Ques: Who are you to give her the door?

ISSIAH: I have the key to the door. I open the door and she will go through now. She will speak, wait.

Breathing slowly

Hmmm

Pause

JIT: I am in a laboratory. I go through the door and it is so bright; I am blinded by the light, just like looking into sunlight. Then I go in further and I can see what looks like the human brain clamped at a table. I can see wire tied to the brain and up to the ceiling, creating access to all areas. There are hands and arms visible to me, working on the brain with long thin instruments.

Ques: 4 sets of hands?

JIT: I am being told it is preparation. I can see beautiful rainbows in the distance. I can see the swirling turquoise and the Orbies are talking to me.

JIT: There is a wolf.

JIT: I am sitting on a high stool at the table; the brain is here. What I perceive to be a brain. Beyond that I can see a big glass window that leads to a path.

JIT: I feel that whatever they are doing to the brain, it is also being replicated somewhere else. The work done on these tables is all part of the bigger picture. There are other TV screens in the room, and each has a picture of a brain on it. The work they do to the brain on the table is also happening to the screen brains.

JIT: This brain, I am told, can be programmed to be anyone's brain in the universe.

Pause

JIT: This reprogramming and tweaking happens to a percentage of the population in preparation for new beginnings. The Orbies are projecting the hands to show me what they are actually doing.

JIT: Preparing for the future.

?: Seen enough- this is the voice of one of the other Orbies

Pausing

JIT: They are telling me I have seen enough; a door opposite to the one I came in is being opened for me to walk through.

JIT: The Orbies are saying I am Intergalactical. I sense a mist on me, a watery kind of a mist.

JIT: I am in the garden with the children, the happy garden. They say they are preparing for the future.

Pausing here

JIT: Never fear yesterday, it is gone; never fear tomorrow, you don't know what it is. To survive in the beautiful garden homeland, you must live in the now. There is no other way, you must. There is no other way.

Nothing will be eradicated from your mind; you will have memory. But you live in the now so the memory is just that, a memory.

ISSIAH: I am Issiah. I will give you more information, later.

Ques: Thank you Issiah.

JAN:

This was quite a factual session with not much emotion. I felt as though I was able to speak as me in trance and to project the voice of Issiah. Giving us an insight into the Universal happenings, perhaps? To come out of this trance humbled to be given insight into life beyond life, to share with you all.

■ ■ ■

Guilt Mirror

24-Feb-2015

Present in the room

JIT: Jan in trance

001: Jan as the spirit/soul voice

Ques: Asking the questions

?: Different person speaking

Reference to home is the spirit world.

Jan makes herself comfortable and begins to take herself into her altered trance state for this connection to channel their voice.

JAN: My eyes are closed as I move into an altered state. I see in my mind's eye a big full length mirror in front of me, maybe 6ft tall, with a wide gilt ornate frame.

JAN: Imagine I am watching a movie; I see lots of white light coming from the left and a train on a track going behind the mirror, but not inside it. I know I need to look in the mirror, but for some reason I can't.

Long pause

Eyes still closed and waiting

JIT: I am just looking where to go, I am asking to be shown and I take deep breaths to take me further into trance.

JIT: There is resistance to go into the mirror, so I am just waiting. I know I need to go in there.

Ques: Is George with you?

(George appears now and again in trance sessions.)

JIT: Yes, he is to the right of me, but I am not George.

JIT: Oh, I see. I had to wait for everything to be lined up; it is lined up now and I can go into the mirror. The face of the mirror has turned black. I feel I will go in the middle of it. I can still see the gilt edge; it is brighter and glistens. I am being pulled closer to the face of the mirror now...

JIT: I can see a vortex in the middle of it.

Jan takes deep breaths and slows her breathing to take her down towards the mirror

JIT: I am going now and leaving George behind; he is urging me in...

JIT: What an intense feeling of energy change as I go through, but not in one go; backwards and forwards I go, but further in each time. I have done it; I have gone through the mirror. All I can see is black; I can see nothing. Looking behind I know the mirror is there.

A different person is communicating

?: I told you she would come and have a look. I told you she would come through, and she has been here before. Come on Jan, come and have a look closer.

Jan breathes deeper and slower

JIT: Star of David.

JIT: I can sense someone holding my hand. I am not flying but I am not walking either. What a strange feeling because there is no floor; I am floating. I am behind the person holding my hand and it is still black.

Very calm energy around Jan

Ques: Do you know who is holding your hand?

JIT: No, I feel it is male energy, but it is not George; he is on the other side of the mirror. I am going further and deeper but it is slow motion. I can sense a path going to the left, and I can sense structures in front to the right. I am moving but I am not going anywhere.

Breathes lower

JIT: Things are floating around; I see a bike. I am in a space; I can see the garden on the other side of some buildings.

Ques: Is it a safe garden?

JIT: Yes.

Breathes lower

JIT: It is opening up and they are telling me they wanted to make sure I was comfortable and to trust me. We are telepathically communicating.

It is all quiet in the room now

JIT: There are lots of random visuals which become more intense when I am quiet. I can see the library that I have seen about before, and I can see the massive books. I say a room, but there is no floor; it is a space and everyone in there is absorbing information.

JIT: The Orbies come and go.

Ques: Hologram?

JIT: I can see a TV screen similar to the other ones, and I can see the brain room. I have more Orbies with me now as they take me though another door. I go past the garden and further down the path.

Lots of quiet… smiles from Jan as she hears the Orbies telepathically communicating

JIT: I can see clusters of coloured Orbies, pinks and orange, green, yellow and purple. Each cluster is telepathically chattering; I hear their words.

JIT: I am told to observe; the Orbie that was leading me is now moving away. The spheres are grouped together by colour and they do not interact outside of their colour group.

JIT: I can see a red Orbie coming to one of the groups; it takes three of them into the room with the TV.

JIT: I am sensing resistance, a bit scared.

JIT: One of the three...

JIT: Just resistance...

JIT: An Orbie sits and projects authority, but not how we know it.

Ques: Is that the red one?

JIT: No, it doesn't have a colour. I can see through it; it is translucent with an opaque edge.

JIT: We are watching the TV screen, and the three Orbies and the opaque one talk. They are talking about going to earth to learn their lessons.

JIT: On the screen I can see a life on earth, a play. I feel they are in the play; this indicates they are being shown what they are going to earth to experience.

Number 1 – A red Orbie will go to earth and live with an exceptionally jealous woman; he will have his own business, and three children with one set of twins. He will experience a heart attack and become depressed. This Orbie will return home at the age of 32.

The red Orbie seems happy; he will experience many things from birth to meeting his partner. I feel his mum will have breast cancer. He will be a troubled soul; at 18 he has a near fatal accident, near because he is rescued by the angels. (Divine intervention)

Number 2 - A red Orbie will be a boy. On the TV screen he is a foetus; as he is born his mum goes home. He will be raised by his sister. He is shown to himself as a child and has no shoes on, brown skin and a smile on his face. His sister wraps her head up. Every night they have a different place to live, a different shelter.

He sits on the kerb and watches the people, everybody likes him. He has no father and likes to please people. One day he runs across the road, and everything goes black for him.

Number 3 - A red Orbie watches the screen and is shown her birth into a family with mum and dad and two sisters. She is happy and likes to dance and sing; she is very carefree. Mother has a favourite and it is her; the others don't like it and show jealously. The favourite is bullied. The favourite dances, sings, swims, runs and jumps. The favourite is tired. The favourite likes the flowers on the coffin.

Ques: Likes the flowers on the coffin?

JIT: She cuts her wrists and she can see the life before she is born. Their life is observed on the screen; when they come to earth they do have déjà vu moments. One of them will be helped by the angels, and they will all live their life to the fullest and will return home. The dates they are agreeing to are their going home dates and nothing will change this. Medical intervention or anything else will not change it.

JIT: The three reds move away from the screen and back to the other reds in their cluster.

JIT: Opaque Orbie sits for a minute and I sense it talking to a higher being, as though it is reporting back. Moving away from that screen-setting, it soon disappears to leave black space as before.

JAN:

As I began to come out of the trance, I realised how intense this one was and so deep, very much beyond earthly words. It brings tears to my eyes when I read it, inside I have the depth of knowing that home, is beyond our descriptive words.

I had to ask Ques to release me. She grounded (grounding is a term used in this work, that keeps you earthly) me and talked me back into the room. She said my eyes looked pink when I opened them.

It took me a while to recover from this session.

Did you notice that there is little interaction with Ques in this session?

We have been shown the Orbies in their land and some of the processes they go through to come to earth, for their learning experiences in a human body.

■ ■ ■

270215

27-Feb-2015

Present in the room

JIT: Jan in trance

Soul: Jan as the baby soul

MAN: Jan as the man

Ques: Asking the questions

Reference to home is the spirit world.

Jan makes herself comfortable and begins to take herself into her altered trance state for this connection to channel their voice.

JIT: Don't be greedy *Are the first words spoken*

(Jan could not settle and had to change her position in the room Pausing while Jan enters her correct altered state.)

JIT: Don't be greedy, I want to tell you a story.

(Jan thinks she has George with her; he is to her right and is there to help her. There is no clarity on George at this point, remember he randomly pops in and out of the sessions.)

Jan smiles

JIT: A beautiful garden with the most amazing colours. Green is the greenest green I have ever seen. I can see flowers, just unearthly flowers; the beautiful mixture of colours and brightness. Everything is so bright.

JIT: I am not going into the garden, just walking past and admiring the flowers and colours.

JIT: As I walk down the path past the garden, I look back; the garden has gone, and I sense it as a hologram. Walking along the path, it feels like I am going downhill; I can see the library where I have been before with the huge books. Someone is reading the one on the table, and they look at me and smile; as I look back and the library has gone.

JIT: I am walking past the brain room. As I continue ,I am told to wait. I am still on the same path. I have to wait; I am told to wait.

Long pause, deep breaths to take Jan deeper into her altered state

Quietly spoken

JIT: I am being taken into a room/space.

JIT: Projected onto the wall in the space are earthly pictures; there are four projections. The projections might be from a camera aimed at earth. That is the impression it gives.

The spheres are given the name Orbies

JIT: Orbies are communicating telepathically. I can hear/understand as they are looking at the pictures on the wall of the earthly things. They are aware of me in the room and George is standing outside on the path. I am told to enter further into the room. (George appears again.)

The following is said at speed and with an urgency

On screens

JIT: I can see scenes from earth. I see people on the streets going about their daily lives. There is a woman with a pushchair and I can see someone coming out of a pub who is drunk.

JIT: We are following the path of a man, going back in time. The man came home late the night before; his wife is there, she is shouting at him for coming in late. Because they argued that led to them sleeping in separate rooms. Their Arguments follow on from the night before; he does not go to work that day. The man walks out of the house and he goes to the pub.

JIT: Drinking and chatting with his friends, all of a sudden he changes position and stands at the side of the bar; his facial expressions show sadness. One drink after another he takes. He decides it is time to leave the bar. He staggers out of the door, eventually reaching the car park.

JIT: Opening the door, he falls into his car. Driving out of the car park to the top of the road, and then he turns left. All of a sudden his foot slips and presses on the accelerator at the exact same time as the woman with the pushchair is on the zebra crossing. The car speeds up even though he tries to brake. The car smashes into the pushchair.

Pause all this is being projected on a screen for Jan to articulate

Everything is said at speed

JIT: We are going back in time and following the path of the mum and her baby. The mum wakes and gets up in the morning. She prepares the baby's bottles for the day and feeds her baby. In the house there is relaxing music playing; the baby is changed and placed in the pram. She must take her out again because she vomits; the baby is changed into fresh clothes and bedding, and they are now ready to go out.

Mum opens the door and realises she has forgotten something, so she returns to the kitchen to collect it from the table. It is a sunny day and they continue their walk; she waves to a friend in the distance and stops for a short natter, then continued on her way. Someone else shouts to her and they exchange a wave. She begins to cross the road at the zebra crossing but they don't get to the other side... The car crashes into the pushchair.

Pauses

I am still looking on the screen and at the mum's house

JIT: We are rewinding in time to the mum's house with the child. As I go into the house I see that mum decided to go back to bed and have some extra sleep.

JIT: Eventually waking up a little late she showered, washed her hair.

JIT: The next scene is her drying her hair; she tries to use straighteners but has forgotten to plug them in and consequently they are cold. She plugs them in now and after getting a few things ready she goes back and straightens her hair.

JIT: The baby is still asleep and has to be woken up; there seems to be a need to go out at a certain time for an appointment. The baby is given her bottle, very quickly. She tries to save time by giving her half but the baby cries as she is hungry and wants more. The baby vomits when laid down in the pram. All bedding and clothing have to be changed.

JIT: Finally, ready, she speaks to a neighbour for far too long, because they had not seen each other for a while. She continued on her way. Waved to someone else she knew across the road.

Had she not fallen back to sleep.

Had she turned the straighteners on.

Had she not tried to rush the baby.

Had she not nattered for too long with the first person. She would not have been at the crossing at the time of impact.

Still being projected on the screen

JIT: Rewinding back in time to the house of the man who is drunk.

JIT: The evening before the accident he decided to go out for a drink with friends and stayed out later than he normally does. His wife was angry that he stayed out so late, which led to arguments.

JIT: At breakfast the atmosphere was still argumentative; he **chose** not to go to work that day and headed to the pub. He really enjoyed chatting to the people who he had not seen for a while. He suddenly had this overwhelming sense of guilt and he moved away to stand on his own. The drink began to flow as he drowned his sorrows. After realising he was drinking too much, he felt remorse and decided to go and buy flowers for his wife and surprise her when she got home from work.

He reached the zebra crossing and crashed.

Pause

JIT: The emergency services begin to arrive, blue lights flashing and sirens screaming to get out of the way.

Remember I am still looking at this on screen

JIT: Paramedics are quickly assessing the scene, the baby and mum are in one ambulance and the man in the other.

Pauses

JIT: Arriving at hospital, the baby is in a very poorly state; the medics are performing compressions on her tiny chest. Sobbing and crying outside of the room in the corridor, mum is distraught with worry. They stop the compressions…

A short pause; there is no feeling or emotion with the words

JIT: In this room there is a mist all around the ceiling and it seems to be coming from the corner of the room.

JIT: My angle of vision is being altered; I can look from the ceiling down to the bed where the baby lays. The soul is rising.

JIT: I feel I am the soul; my angle of vision has changed again.

Jan is the soul of the baby

Soul: I am guided to go to the corner of the room where most of the mist is. I have muted yellows and purples and lots of white energy around me.

Soul: A beautiful bright energy, but not a specific bright white light. As the soul, I feel like I am rising. I see a door made of Perspex; I can see what I know are my soul group family on the other side of the door. As I turn to the right, the door opens; I am so happy, I feel warmth and content, just home.

Soul: Lots of Orbies in different colours; orange, red, green and a white one. It is the white one that comes forward and we go off together into a winding corridor with no walls. I can see a path. I have the mist around me. I can see no human forms.

I feel happy inside, and muted

Soul: We arrive in the garden, but this time I do not see the colours of the flowers; everything is muted whites and greys with a bench in the middle. I sit on the bench and feel a presence sitting next to me; the other Orbies are moving away and leaving us together. I am not sitting as in human form, I just know.

Soul: I am welcomed home as I look at the flowers' silvery petals and grey foliage. Over in the corner, I can see the flowers changing; they are coming alive with colour. Almost as though they were being magically painted. In the same corner is a void and I see more Orbies coming in, drenching the flowers in colour.

Soul: Everything feels clean, as in the opposite of dirty. Dirty is behind me and I am in the clean. It feels like the bad has gone and I am in the good. The warm against the cold, so reassuringly calm and positive.

Soul: Overwhelmed by the feelings of being able to communicate with the Orbies, third eye connection. Their third eye, eye to eye.

I want to touch my third eye as I look at theirs

Soul: All the Orbies are milling around, a fashionable cocktail party would describe it well. But there is no floor and there are no legs, just wonderful Orbies, Spherical intelligence of the telepathic Galaxy, a sophisticated party atmosphere. All calm, very calm, so calm.

Soul: Telepathy is chatter but not noisy chatter, knowing chatter. We all know, but we are not actually talking.

I have left the baby soul; I am back to JIT

Speaks quickly

JIT: As I have left the soul I begin to move along a path and I see another place off to the left. Everything seems to be off to the left. I take a look back and everything I have just experienced is no longer there. It has all gone from my vision.

JIT: I can see a similar room to that which I have seen before with the earth connection, and this is further along the path.

MAN: We are being shown the hospital from the man's perspective now.

MAN: Banging his head, the man is injured; looking on the screen I can see he omitted to put his seatbelt on when he left the pub. As he braked so hard when he crashed his head lunged forward onto the steering wheel.

MAN: The x-ray machine is being brought over; he has to have a MRI scan too. I see him shaking in the tube, returning to the medical room where he has numerous medical doctors and nurses around him.

JIT: From the void in the corner of the room; I sense an angelic being. I say that because I can see what look like floaty pieces of fabric coming into the room; they position themselves around the bed. There are six. They are around the man, hovering above the heads of the doctors.

JIT: As they are looking over the man, I see an Orbie enter the room. As the soul leaves the body, it travels to the corner of the room.

JIT: The angelic beings float around and retrieve the soul from the corner, replacing it into the body. Doctors and nurses who were unable to help are chattering and showing relief because the man will go on to live the rest of his human life.

JIT: As I glide along the path and look back, everything has disappeared.

I am still watching on a screen

JIT: This room/space with a screen is similar to the others; I am in the man's house before he went out.

JIT: His wife had gone out with friends and she thought he was staying in. However, he did go out. A friend called; I can see him on the phone. His friend persuaded him to go out. He finds it difficult to say no and likes to please everyone, so he joined the others in the pub.

JIT: It did feel more like a club; everyone was drinking and happy with loud music playing. He kept looking at his watch and thinking that he must go. As he went to leave, everyone asked him to stay a little longer.

JIT: Not wanting to let them down, he stayed; the more he drank the less he thought about the time and his wife who assumed he was in the house. In the early hours, he went home.

JIT: He felt shame as he had not thought about his wife at home wondering where he was.

JIT: This was the scenario that led to the arguments that have already been described.

The screen is fast forwarding the next few scenes

JIT: Man getting better in hospital very fast, fast forward.

His wounds are dressed, his medication is collected and he leaves the hospital.

Still fast forwarding

JIT: Going home to his wife.

JIT: Wife not happy; they are arguing. I am being shown his life normal with everyday things going on.

I feel his wife is still not happy.

I feel his wife leaves him.

He tries to go out with his old friends.

They don't want him.

He is miserable.

He is home alone and very sad.

He becomes ill.

Does not want to go out.

Stays in the house.

Starts to drink.

Becomes a recluse.

Everything on screen is fast, fast forwarding in time

JIT: He stops taking care of himself.

JIT: He stops cleaning the house.

Long pause

Deep breaths to change

JIT: I see from his perspective and take on his persona.

Very slowly spoken, with sadness

MAN: I feel really ill; I feel sick; what's the point of life? I have no friends and my family ignore me. I have no money and people are always banging on the door.

Sometimes they put letters through and ask for money, but I have no money. I cannot pay.

MAN: I have a void that feels like a big hole in my heart. No one is listening to me. I have never listened to myself. I always pleased and looked after everyone else; I gave them what they wanted. It did not enter my head to think about what I wanted.

Self-talking

MAN: Do I want this?

MAN: NO.

MAN: How do I get out of this? I have conversations with myself every day. How do I get out of this?

Pause and exhales in disgust

MAN: I have some tablets, and some whiskey. I do like whiskey; there isn't much left though. I can't afford any more and there is enough to wash the tablets down; I will feel alright. On the kitchen table is the whiskey and eight tablets; I pour the whiskey into the glass and look at the tablets. I pick them up in my hand.

MAN: I start to cough and I become angry inside. The anger rises and I release it by throwing the glass at the wall, leaving the tablets in my hand. I look at them and think...

Breathes deeply

MAN: What are you doing?

The voice is very quiet now

MAN: I open the curtains and look out of the window; there is no one there and I have no friends. No one wants me. Everyone liked me when I helped them and gave them things. Opening the door in the kitchen to go outside and take a walk in the garden to breathe some air, I remembered there is some rope in the shed.

Deep in thought; something changes and the voice becomes more upbeat

MAN: At this point I feel quite happy and on top of things, more so than in a while. The fresh air is giving me a new perspective on life. Even the neighbour shouts *hello* and comments that he hasn't seen me for a while. He also asks what I am doing with the rope. I inform him that I am going to tie something up in the tree as I continue down the garden.

Breathes and sighs

Even more upbeat now

MAN: I'm feeling excited, with that knowing feeling that something good is about to happen.

MAN: I can hear my dad talking and he died years ago; I am a little bemused to hear his voice and that old dog we used to have I hear barking in the distance.

MAN: What's all this coming into my head for?

He asks himself this question

MAN: I hear a baby crying; I will never forget that cry. It is the baby my wife and I lost.

I feel happy and question it

MAN: I have a sense of happiness hearing the familiar past. Why do they make me feel happy?

Everything seems to be in slow motion now

MAN: The other day I left a ladder up against the old gnarled oak tree. I climb up the strongest branches, reaching out like long arms to the happy place.

JIT: When I see the arms in my mind's eye, the branches lengthened and the vibrations changed.

The man rests for a minute

MAN: Sitting in the tree, I look around and notice the skyline and scenery has changed to show me lots of beautiful colours. I know it is time to tie up the tree with the special knots they have shown me. I am being told to throw the rope over the branch and let the loose ends dangle.

Has a conversation with the voices in his head

MAN: I put the necklace on. I don't usually wear necklaces. You can wear this one, they tell me. It is very heavy, like the honour of being mayor and wearing the gold and red chain for special duties.

MAN: I can hear my father calling me…

Father: Come home son, come home… come on…

Softly spoken

MAN: I leap out of the tree, and I go home.

MAN: I have this wonderful sense of peace and knowing. As I near a room, someone opens the door and I see my father and the baby… I am so very happy, and the dog…

MAN: I know the voice and I go towards her; we are so happy to see each other. Ecstatic, it is so overwhelming to be home again. So very beautiful to feel the luxury of not being in that vehicle. Released.

Breathes and takes in surroundings

Breathes deeper and sounds exhausted

Pauses

JIT: I am on the path again. The energy around me feels amazing, wonderful. To be in the right place at the right time and everything is good. I am being pulled to the path although I want to stay in that energy.

JIT: The next room is a TV room and I have to go in; George is there and staying on the path.

JIT: On the TV screen we are going back in time into the house of the MAN. He was never meant to go to hospital that day; a chain of events with people's choices and experiences led to it. (Divine intervention/free-will)

JIT: This man was always refusing to be the person that he came to earth to be. His earthly personality consisted of wanting to always help other people and his choices led him to be a yes man. Living his life for others. He didn't realise that he could live for himself and still help others. The fact that he did not do it this way brought about the changes at home, the voices in his head, the depression that made him stay in the house.

JIT: His life ended in the way that was agreed before being born; it was his natural ending.

JIT: The TV screen is fast rewinding to before he was born and clarifying that he decided what he was going to do on earth, and how long he would stay for including how he would return home.

JIT: The tree and mayor's chain/rope as the necklace is how he was always going back home.

JIT: Fast forward now to the operating room in the hospital when I saw the fabric angelic people coming down and giving him his soul back. This is what we call divine intervention. He was never going to die in the accident.

JIT: He used to dream of being a Mayor as a child. So he fulfilled his contract with divine intervention.

JIT: I am on to the path now and George is holding my arm. I can see the garden; he is by my side and saying he will call for me again; he thanks me.

JIT: I feel a sense of reversing to where I need to be; George has gone.

JAN:

This was a very deep trance and lasted for 52 minutes. As I came back, I had a wonderful sense of achievement with love and contentment washing over me. I felt very floaty and could not open my eyes easily; my body was in the room but my thoughts were not.

To be given insight into the different scenarios of the man and the woman shows how our lives are and can be changed by the slightest reaction. I imagine you can think of times in your life that would have been so different if you altered the way you said or did something. As they come into your mind, pop them in your notebook for referencing later.

■ ■ ■

5456

28-Feb-2015

Present in the room

JIT: Jan in trance

GOLDO: Jan as Gold Orbie

EarthO: Jan as Earth Orbie, ones that are returning to earth

Ques: Asking the questions

Reference to home is the spirit world.

Jan makes herself comfortable and begins to take herself into her altered trance state for this connection to channel their voice.

JIT: I feel like I am being turned.

JIT: That's it, I am going now.

Jan breathes deeper

JIT: I am ready.

JIT: I keep getting the word *aubergine*; that is where I have to start. I feel a bit all over the place, I keep seeing the path I saw yesterday when it goes I am taken up to a bright white cloud-like mass. Just a mass of white.

JIT: Not really going anywhere yet, but seeing things.

JIT: Whoever is coming to help in on the right hand side, and I sense it is George. Perhaps they will tell me who it is.

Ques: Is it not George?

JIT: I don't know; I feel I know him but not as in a relative. He will tell me later, they are telling me to shut up and let it happen…

JIT: I have big tickles on my head; it is like they are pushing my head down.

Come on

JIT: I am aware of Notre Dame and I can see a street square, I can see a bit of an old temple. I can see two big pillars with a triangle joining them together on the top. I want to walk through these posts and as I do, I end up underground.

JIT: I walk through the pillars, stand still and I am transported underground.

JIT: All the time I am going underground on this side.

Gestures to the right

I am transported in my mind to the place where I went yesterday. I can see the TV screens. To understand it, I am underground and can see flashes of yesterday. I am just deeper into trance and I feel I need to turn around and see from a different angle.

JIT: Here we go. Now I can see corridors underground and doors going off them. There are doors on the left and right. I can see through one of the doors. I have vision; I can see through them.

JIT: There is a large table with maps of the world on it and little pins in the maps. There are about five people standing around in human form just looking and moving the pins about. They have various monitors in the room, but I cannot see what is on them.

JIT: I have a sense that I am being moved to the corridor. I am on the opposite side further along. In there, I can see six people sitting in chairs, bucket chairs. One person is behind a big desk; everyone is talking, and these words are heard in different places.

JIT: This is a sense from being in the room.

JIT: I don't feel the English language is being spoken.

JIT: I come out into the corridor; in my mind I flick to the TV screen. I can see everything on the TV screen that I have just experienced.

JIT: Walking forward in the corridor, I arrive at a big circular space with six corridors that lead off. I'm going forward again; everything is dark in the corridors and I cannot see the surroundings. I know I am going straight.

JIT: I am not quite sure where I am. I can see people in human form. I want to say pharmaceuticals.

JIT: I can see little white tablets; I feel that pharmaceuticals are controlled by one.

JIT: There are so many dead animals, skeletons of animals, sheep, ewes and bullocks too; something is being tested on the bullocks, and my vision is taken from the animals. I cannot see them now.

JIT: There is a desk in this room. As I go and sit at the desk, I am being turned now to be the person sitting in the desk.

JIT: I am looking through the eyes of someone sitting at the desk.

JIT: I sit in the seat and look forward. I can see monitors. When I look at the monitors, I know they are showing different countries. I see the time is different on each one, there are about eight.

JIT: On the screens I can see laboratories, real physical laboratories. Animal testing, mixing up of powder, microscopes and I can see tablets.

JIT: I am going into a cool store. It is locked, bolted and padlocked. Secured. I am going in. Someone takes out a tray with tubes in it and they place it on the side. There are a lot of tablets. I want to put whatever is in the test tubes into the tablets after they are made.

JIT: Remember, I am in the chair at the desk watching this on the monitors. At the same time, I am experiencing what is on the monitor.

JIT: It is an experiment, but I feel it is more than an experiment. I feel it has already been experimented. I have a syringe and draw up from the test tube and inject it into the tablet.

JIT: I know whoever takes these tablets, whatever these tablets are for, it speeds up something. For example, a tablet given as a cure or remedy but then it speeds up or changes something else inside the person.

Ques: Did you say given as a cure?

JIT: Yes.

JIT: Nothing is as it seems. When I look on all the monitors they show laboratories. The coolroom is locked on all of them, secured and not everyone has access.

JIT: Whatever is in the coolroom is being added to the tablets as described above. The tablets have gone or are going out on trial; I don't feel they are in distribution.

Back with my helper

JIT: I am coming out of that room and walking forward. I seem to stop. Then, I appear in the historical ruins. I walk out of there and don't take much notice of my surroundings.

JIT: I am walking forward and as I look back the ruins have disappeared.

JIT: As I walk forward the vibrations have changed and I am walking into that vibration.

Pause, looking around

JIT: becomes the Gold Orbie

GoldO: I have an overwhelming sense of calm now; I feel peaceful and rested. In the other place, I felt agitated like I had time scales and deadlines. I had schedules to meet. I felt like I was doing something wrong but I was doing something right.

GoldO: I am taking in the atmosphere, being at one. I am not in human form; I feel so much calmer in Orbie state. I can smell something fresh. I just want to stay here and I don't want to move, I don't want to change. It feels lovely; the smell feels lovely.

GoldO: When I experience those beautiful feelings it is like nothing on earth. All senses are greatly exaggerated from what we know on earth.

GoldO: I have still got what I perceive to be a guide with me. I am sure his name is George; it is.

Rubs hands together lots, building up energy in hands

Pause, pause

GoldO: Where am I going now?

GoldO: I can see lots of things hovering around, but nothing specific. I feel so content so relaxed, so at home. I can see the TV screens in the distance to the left.

Take a moment now

GoldO: I feel I am being tested with something; I can't grasp what it is, but I know. I have a knowing and a sensing feeling. This is the only way it can be described.

GoldO: I feel as though my aura has been changed. I feel…

Jan gestures in circles in front of her to suggest this

GoldO: I am not in an earthly body, I am spherical. I want to put my arms around my body as though something has changed in my aura.

GoldO: When I talk about the path and the rooms, the rooms on the left are used by the Orbies and the rooms on the right are used by human form.

GoldO: On the left of the path I am going towards some TV screens which are on the wall facing me. I have never been in this room before, although it is very similar to the other TV rooms. I can see some black and dark green Orbies in here.

GoldO: On the screens I can see a cross section enabling me to see what is going on inside, underground. I can see exactly what I have just been shown in the other room, with human forms.

GoldO: The black and green Orbies are telepathically communicating with each other and moving about, buzzing!

GoldO: I feel like I am being held back, I feel that they don't want to show me. I am telling them it is ok; I am supposed to be here. Now, I see these multiple rows of TV screens each with an Orbie on it, lined up like soldiers. On each TV screen I can see a different section of the underground tunnels.

Ques: CCTV?

GoldO: When I was in the other place with human forms, it was on CCTV monitors. This one is a TV screen. They were watching CCTV. Where I am now, they are TV screens.

Ques: A cross section?

GoldO: But as in TV, on-going and moving; I can see the whole, not one camera. I am looking down from above one of the tunnels.

(Similar to a cross section of a rabbit warren).

GoldO: Each one has a different tunnel.

GoldO: I am being told DNA. On the TV screen I can see the orbs. In the CCTV screens, they are changing the contents of the test tubes.

GoldO: The DNA will be changed with the addition to the tablets.

GoldO: Back to the TV screens and I can see the cupboards being opened by the Orbies. I can now see the Orbies making changes on the table.

GoldO: Whatever is changed on the table is projected on all the TV screens. The TV screen has a cross section of the underground which is like a hologram, projected on the table. Whatever they do on the table is reflected in the monitors.

GoldO: The liquid from the coolrooms are being replaced by the Orbies. The human forms then put the liquid into the tablets. The tablets are then tested and do not have the effect they had planned them to have.

GoldO: Divine intervention has taken place; everything needs to go back to a natural state.

Ques: What, the DNA needed to go back to a natural state?

JIT: Now takes over.

JIT: No, on earth. It will become one.

JIT: We are on the fall. These people on the other side are on the fall; the underground earthlings are on the fall. It is like rise and fall, they are on the fall.

JIT: Divine intervention is needed to create the created, to master the mastered, to voice the voiced, to map the mapped; we are the voice, we are the one.

Jan is being taken out of there

GoldO: I am near another room with the TV screens and Orbies; I am told to go in this room. There are screens on the left and the big screen in front. I am hovering at the back of the room.

GoldO: A large table in the centre of the room with the TV screen in front.

GoldO: Two Orbies are speaking together. One is Silver Toes, and he informs the other one that it is going to earth. I can hear a gentle exchange of voices about what experiences will be experienced. The Orbie going to earth is being told that life won't be that good because it is going to experience the opposite of good. This orb has already experienced a lot of positivity and grandeur in a previous visit to earth.

GoldO: Experience the opposite, of being a victim.

GoldO: Abuse, poverty, loss, extreme cold, mental health; the Orbie knows that this will be one of the most horrendous rebirths it has ever had. The human life is fast forwarded on the screen exactly how it should happen from birth to going back home. It is being shown there will be 3 getaway points.

GoldO: So that is all discussed in a little bit more detail, and I feel like I am becoming that Orbie now.

GoldO: I become the Orbie that is going to earth.

EarthO: I go to this area where there are other Orbies. I know we are all going to be born into human vehicles on earth; I see a cat. One Orbie will be a cat. We are all in the transition space.

EarthO: We are all quite excited and a little apprehensive, looking and telepathically chatting to each other about the information given from Silver Toes. Everyone will be incarnated at the same time.

EarthO: On another screen there are vortexes; each Orbie has its own vortex linked to it, to go to earth. The Orbies just somehow know when it is time to go forward into their space on the screen.

EarthO: As they go forward, each Orbie enters the screen and goes through their vortex. Memory of the spirit world is erased on entry through the vortex.

The switches are not literal switches but to give you a sense of on and off

JIT: Switches are talked about, and they use the word switch to make us understand. The switches will be on or off depending on what each entry to earth has to experience. It is actually a thought process.

JIT: Each Orbie will enter Earth as the following:

1. Victim enters into the vortex.
2. Black kitten enters the vortex.
3. Quite strong mental health, similar to schizophrenia; this will be recognised just before it returns home. For this rebirth not all memory will be erased from previous lives. It will hold the memory of five previous lives, these becoming the mental personalities and voices. Not all the switches were off on entry.

4. Born to riches, grandeur and delight. Life will focus on the arts, vast lands, gold, happiness and creativity.

JIT: I am moving away now as the last one goes through the relevant vortex. We will be shown this in more detail later.

JIT: I can hear them telepathically communicating about the importance of experiencing opposites; the good versus the bad, the right versus the wrong, the easy versus hard, the rich, the poor, the cold, the hot; these experiences enable us to become whole Orbies and move on.

1. The Orbie who is the victim feeling abuse has already experienced a good life.
2. The cat has already experienced a human form and now enters in animal form.
3. The Orbie who goes through to experience schizophrenia will have already experienced doctor, child, astronaut, peasant and king.
4. The Orbie going through this time to experience the gold and riches has previously or will in the future experience loss.

Pausing now

JIT: I am going into another space with screens on the left.

JIT: I know that Codes; formulas and strings of information along with new formula and DNA will be released. The pattern of things to come will change.

JIT: Governments will fall, strengths will weaken and the weak will strengthen; we will become as one. Moving to a common denominator, not everyone will survive. Those that survive will be rewarded with peace and tranquillity, beauty and paradise. Some will not survive; those that are not ready will live on earth forever more.

JIT: I will show you the strings of DNA; the new ones will be recreated in the fields of crops. Look out for the new systems and recognise the subtle changes.

JIT: Did I make sense before? 1 and 1 is not 6. Here is a hint that the sums do not add up. Sort out any confusions with DNA, and formulas will be reflected in the mirror; the correct answers will be shown for the future.

JIT: I am being told to go back now. They will continue with this in the future.

JIT: I feel like I am just whizzing backwards to the path where my friend is.

JIT: Everything, it is backwards. Thank you.

JAN:

This was another very deep experience for me. Everything was so visual and meaningful as the Orbies revealed more. It was clear that the Orbies are able to help and change the actions of humans on earth. Remember, as I am in trance, I actually don't remember what I have said. It is only when I transcribe, that I relive and subsequently have the memory, emotions and feelings. Once transcribed, I am given the sense of having been there.

Very little interaction with Ques.

I am so humbled by this work every day.

■ ■ ■

Jan Mayfield

Black Cat

02-March-2015

Present in the room

JIT: Jan in trance

GoldO: Jan as the Golden Orb

Ques: Asking the questions

Reference to home is the spirit world.

Jan makes herself comfortable and begins to take herself into her altered trance state for this connection to channel their voice.

Almost immediately Jan hears voices asking her where she has been, they have been waiting for her.

JIT: I feel like I have whiskers.

JIT: I feel like I am a black cat. I feel like I have cat whiskers coming out of my face. I feel like I am a cat.

JIT: I can't move forward until I speak what I feel.

JIT: The cat is taking me to the path. I am the cat going to the path.

JIT: It has left me at the path.

JIT: I needed to experience how it felt to be a cat.

JIT: I felt my body grow a back and a tail. I could feel the whiskers too.

All this felt very real to JIT

Long pause as JIT goes deeper

JIT: I have a man coming to the right.

Ques: George?

The question was ignored

JIT: I am from Orbie perspective now.

GoldO: I feel lifted and I am higher than the path and I am looking down, I can see.

GoldO: Imagine you are in a commentator's box at a football ground. The football ground is my path and to the left of it is showing me where I have been.

GoldO: I am being shown the TV screen in the brain room, a library, tablets and garden rooms and they are all on the left side of the path.

There is a barrier across the path; I can see from the higher perspective beyond the barrier, which is a long dark path. I feel I will need to be allowed through the barrier.

GoldO: Back on to the path as Orbie, I am told I am a Gold Orbie.

QUES: What is the significance of Gold Orbie?

GoldO: I have a passkey to open all doors.

Long pause; I have lots of spirit around me - goes deeper into altered state

Speaks in a quiet voice

GoldO: I am at the doorway.

GoldO: There are lots of mirrors, other halves of something… other half of skull, other half of, not a reflection of.

GoldO: I see a wall and it is opening up as I reach it.

GoldO: Big doors opening forward to allow me to go through, and George is with me.

Breathes to go deeper

GoldO: It's so beautiful, a very calm purple; remember there are no floors or walls as such. I hover along; the space is purple today.

Breathes to go deeper

GoldO: I walk along the path.

GoldO: I see 3 stalls, like stables, with lots of Orbies in them. It is a space that is created. The colours are mixed but segregated into three lots like cattle stalls.

Buzzing atmosphere

GoldO: I see Silver Toes in the distance.

GoldO: In the stall close to Silver Toes, an orb goes over and brings someone to Silver Toes.

GoldO: This place is for people/Orbies who have returned home. Soon after, they speak with Silver Toes to discuss their earthly life.

GoldO: Individually, they sit with him and then move off in different directions.

GoldO: I am moved on; when I look back the stalls disappear.

Matter of fact voice

GoldO: Carry on walking.

GoldO: Very black, very purple, very dark with beautiful purple swirls; it is ok to go into the dark.

GoldO: Oh, wow! As I walk forward there is a big flash of light.

Overwhelmed

GoldO: There is a big flash of light and a wet mist is here too.

Takes Jan's breath in awe

The words are slowly spoken as though everything is revealed slowly

GoldO: The wet mist goes and I can see a control room; it is so big it goes way into the distance. I can see a space inside it. The Orbies look tiny because they are so far away; judging on size, it is a long way off and I see into the space..a massive screen and then the Orbies are... urm.

GoldO: There are spaces for them to be, to look at the screen.

GoldO: I can hear the words *control, deliverance* and *systematic*. They are taking me there; the orbs are getting bigger as we draw closer. I am not on a path; I am in a space.

Paused

Ques: Is Silver Toes there?

Does not want to be interrupted

GoldO: No. It is so beautiful. I am there now and in the space, the control room.

GoldO: There is a pulse and I see a black dot; the black dot is pulsating and vibrating/beating.

GoldO: There is a big screen, but I can't work it all out; I feel they are blanking some of it from my sight, so I don't see it all.

GoldO: On the screen, there are babies- like a maternity ward on earth with all the little cots.

GoldO: Projecting on screen to a maternity ward. I can see babies, and midwives are around. I can see babies being born but there are other hazy parts on the screen I am not to see.

GoldO: Birth and babies is the main feature. I see it as an infinite number of babies being born. The birth.

GoldO: I **know** that these babies being born are all in a different place, I know it is not one place like a hospital. They do not seem to show the where, roads, paths, hospitals etc.

GoldO: All I see are the births on the screen.

A long pause

GoldO: There are a lot of Orbies in this space. They are not all looking at the screen; they have instruments in front of them on what looks like a desk.

GoldO: What they are doing on their desks/tables is what happens at the births. They are working on earth through the screens.

GoldO: Control.

I sense they are controlling something to do with the births

GoldO: Manifesting ourselves on earth, we control.

Breathes deep and pauses

GoldO: I see they have stopped the screen at a baby coming out; they are not moving forward. It may be hidden from me.

GoldO: So the babies are recreating themselves, birthing themselves.

GoldO: They are birthing themselves but they are still Orbies.

GoldO: Fine-tuned. Soul control.

GoldO: I am being moved out of that space.

JIT: Deep breathing and seems like all is finished

There is silence and then in a meaningful voice

GoldO: I have been soul controlled

QUES: Who are you?

GoldO: Golden Orb

QUES: Is it a good thing to be soul controlled?

GoldO: Good?

GoldO: We endeavour to make earth a peaceful place.

GoldO: We endeavour to change the planet's atmospherics.

GoldO: We endeavour to change the people's voice, the people's attitude.

GoldO: We endeavour to change the people.

GoldO: We endeavour to change, what has already been changed.

GoldO: You see.

JIT: The soul projects its soul; these are a chosen few. It is like soul casting, and you choose the soul.

JIT: The old souls, the souls nearing completion, will be the ones that are chosen.

JIT: The one you call *Jan* has just seen the souls.

JIT: The soul birth. The double soul. The soul mirror. Many different ways this has been described.

JIT: We will show you the soul as the soul watches the birthing of the soul.

JIT: I am showing you now, as we move along the path I will take you to the next place and you will see… come.

Breathes deeper and mumbles to self

JIT: The soul is contained in the little space that I am showing you; the soul is contained. The soul has its own screen to watch its soul birth.

JIT: There are many soul corners where souls will be doing this; remember it is the old souls.

JIT: They see the birth, but they control the birth; they control the soul, they guide the soul, they deliver the soul, they amuse the soul.

JIT: This has been planned many times over; it has been planned to perfection. We only deal with perfection and precise intervention.

JIT: This soul will do no wrong, this soul will merge amongst the people and this soul will never be known. As you say recluse, loner, black sheep, never integrating as others do.

Breathes deeper; this is a very deep, intensely meaningful connection

JIT: You can see on the screen the life of the soul, the reflected soul, the copy soul; we don't have a name you will have a name.

QUES: What is the earth name?

JIT: Some people say earth angel, but it is beyond; it is beyond earth angel, it is beyond eccentric, it is beyond guru, it is beyond, beyond. No one ever really knows the true value of that soul on earth; they never really understand that soul.

JIT: So you see we work that soul.

The soul works the soul. As we begin the process of creating a more peaceful path.

This is a different, more upbeat voice

JIT: Come on then, we can't stop here; come on then, follow me. Here we are, look, here is the next place.

Long pause

JIT: Here are the red ones and here are the orange ones.

JIT: Creating history, creating a future, creating the thoughts. The orange and the red deliver the thoughts to those earthlings who need to be guided more.

JIT: The red and the orange are your inner mind.

JIT: The reds and the oranges give you the thoughts.

JIT: The thoughts all come from here; it is the reds and oranges that give you the thoughts; not your thoughts, our thoughts. We give you the thoughts to think.

A pause is taken

JIT: We only do this for the special ones, the ones that will make progress in their lives on earth. You see, not everyone on earth is there to make peace. Not everyone is there to build the future, not everyone is there to show love and compassion, not everyone is there for this. Not in this lifetime, different lifetimes.

JIT: We build the future now; we build the future.

JIT: Look.

JIT: Look at the connection between the orange and the red. On the screen you see beyond, that is earth, that is an earthling. That earthling has lost its way; that earthling used free-will. We will now create a situation to make that earthling go back on the path that it should have been on. Free-will only goes so far, you know.

JIT: People talk about free-will as if it is a gift. *Well I have free-will, I can do this; well I have free-will, I can do that.* You will always get brought back to where we want you to be.

A long pause

JIT: Do you understand this?

Ques: Are you speaking to me?

JIT: Yes.

JIT: You may question now.

Ques: What do I need to know?

A long silence

JIT: No questions?

Ques: I don't know what to ask.

The voice has a concerned tone to it

JIT: Do you understand in your earthly mind?

Ques: Yes, I do understand in the earthly mind.

JIT: Then forward we will go.

A pause

A pause

JIT: Taking the golden orb higher and higher for observation.

JIT: The golden orb will then speak of what it sees.

JIT: The golden orb is rising now.

JIT: The golden orb is rising high.

JIT: I am placing the golden orb, high.

JIT: When the golden orb is ready, we will switch the vision from me to the golden orb

Ques: Who are you?

Speaks quietly

JIT: We are switching. Wait a moment.

Pause and deep breaths and connection is made

GoldO: We are sitting on the moon and I can see a **vast** expanse of nothingness, in the nothingness I can see…

Pauses, overwhelmed

Voice speeds up now

GoldO: I can see interconnecting stratospheric mind-absorbing visual connectors. Through these, I see the energy as pulsating blocks of various colours and different thicknesses with their own vibration.

GoldO: I observe as the single Orbies are looking at their screens and sending information to their soul; I look as the birthing Orbies are sending information to the mother. I look as there are vast amounts of similar stations just pivoting in what looks like space, but I know they are not far from earth.

GoldO: They are just pivoting there for me to see; they all work differently but as one.

GoldO: Many signals come out of the earth to reach up and out and round and into the Orbies' thought pattern's vibration. Vibrations are all picked up and acted upon by the Orbies. Through the lines and grids that I see, the coils that I see and are taken to earth. Sitting hovering high above, earth to my left and Orbies to my right, I can swivel in the chair and see all around me. There is so much more to see and feel and know. So much more to know.

JIT: So we are taken down to earth.

All said in a matter of fact way

GoldO: I am in a shop somewhere in the world; someone who comes in with a gun and shoots me.

As I am shot, the singular Orbies are watching the other part of their soul in the little stalls that we saw before. They send something through the lines to that person's soul to fetch it back.

GoldO: And the soul comes back to the homeland very quickly. It goes to the stall/stable with the soul watching the screen and it merges as one. The screen closes and then that Orbie just hovers somewhere else. That body then on earth disappears. No one has seen or heard the shooting. No one misses the shooting, but I know that whatever the person was put on earth to do is complete.

Breathes a sigh

JIT: Back up as JIT, with overwhelming calmness and beautiful feelings, knowing at once, and I am coming down the path, coming back the other way and walking forwards; George is with me. As I am going back along the path, looking behind and everything is not there; even the purple has gone now.

JIT: I am guided to go to the garden.

JAN:

There is an abrupt end to the connection and I quickly come out of the session, but I am not alert. I felt that

I wanted to stay as I had this overwhelming sense of happiness and contentment.

There was little interaction with Ques and you will have noticed there was a missed opportunity to question GoldO. Perhaps there was a lack of understanding of what was happening.

■ ■ ■

Black Dot

03-March-2015

Present in the room

JIT: Jan in trance

GOLDO: Jan as Golden Orb

Ques: Asking the questions

Reference to home is the spirit world.

Jan makes herself comfortable and begins to take herself into her altered trance state for this connection to channel their voice.

JIT: Magnitude of the cerebral inclusions is yet to be accessed. Show me the way? I hear you say. We are here for guidance only; certain people will be given information regarding formulas and access codes. As the time draws closer, we will show you in daylight and dawning.

Pause

JIT: We hold the keys to the doors! We hold the keys to open the doors.

JIT: Glasgow is the place. Open your eyes to see that connection to Glasgow.

JIT: Multifaceted, look under the microscope to see the multifaceted ice formations. The answers you search for will be shown reflected in the mirror, one half of the formula you have; the other is reflection. I have it all, I have the mirror.

Ques: Who are you?

JIT: I will show you.

Pause and very slow speech

JIT: Allow me to make it right for you. As we join forces we will become one to feel the pain; there is no pain. To feel the love, there is no love. To feel emotion, but there is no emotion; deliverance is key.

Ques: Who will you join forces with?

Ignores the question

Long pause again; I can see pictures and colours

JIT: I am in the homeland waiting; I want you to be with me. I wait for you to realise, realisation, visualisation and dynamite.

Pause again here, but I can see beauty

JIT: The stringed quartet plays the music of the soul; do you hear the stringed quartet's vibrations resonate through space?

JIT: Jan's journey of discovery will become worldwide knowledge as she shares the information I impart to her. The people will never question, they listen. The right people will receive, read and understand the words you channel.

JIT: Previous lives gained knowledge and understanding with commitment to enable you to be here today. Hard work is always rewarded, with new rewards being shown soon.

Pause

JIT: Look for a connection to brown leather. It is a key to open doors in the future. Once all the doors have been opened, your journey will also be complete with us. This experience is for you alone and will not be repeated anywhere else.

JIT: Send out the clues of life's crossword of infinitum; add together the sums that are already there to give the answers to the sums that people are looking for.

Voice changes now to loud and strong

JIT: Dangerously low on resources, I hear someone say; there is no danger as nothing is dangerously low. Everyone is given the right amount of resources.

JIT: Resources can be physical, spiritual and knowledge.

Pause

Becomes Gold Orb

GoldO: I find myself on the chair, there is a room to the right with the TV screens in it; I see from a different angle as I sit at the opposite end of the path. This is an all seeing chair. To the right is a hologram room where I will move to soon. As I look along the path, there are the same spaces showing different scenarios on the TV.

GoldO: There are concerns on earth!

I am going off on a tangent

GoldO: All TVs are honing in on earth's black dot. I do not know what the black dot is. I hear telepathically that someone on earth is trying to change important things.

GoldO: The black dot is... One of the leaders on earth.

Give me a moment

GoldO: The black dot is getting bigger but I need to see in it. I am asking if this is possible.

GoldO: A leader of an area on earth has changed something out of their remit.

GoldO: The Orbies are intervening on... I am told I am not to share it, all I can say is it is palatial intervention.

Speaking as JIT

JIT: I am being ushered into a space, the room with the next TV in it. I don't have George with me but just before I reach the room, a new Orbie appears and helps me.

JIT: I see a ginormous bright purple light that feels very powerful. The light has morphed into a huge eye, down to the fullest detail.

JIT: I am going down to a communication space; I have to wait outside. All the areas that I can see in are becoming opaque. I know I am not to know any more about the black dot on earth.

I feel quite comfortable with that. I have had eyes before; I know it is telepathy. I am calling it 'third eye speaking.'

JIT: I receive colours from the new Orbie presence opposite me; I take a moment to look around.

Long pause

JIT: Moving along the path, I see another TV space. As I look behind, that room has not disappeared as all others have done before.

JIT: The seriousness of the other room is not reflected in this one. I hover, taking in the layout. Each corner has a podium; a group of Orbies are entering. I sense they want to talk as they place me in the room.

JIT: The time has come to make decisions; I am being given the option to carry on with them or stop at this point. I agree to write everything I am given to help other people. I have to share globally and they give me the number 100,000. I do not know what the number is for at this point.

JIT: Becoming a Gold Orbie gives me full access to visit when I want but equally they can call on me. To be given all the keys too, I feel very honoured.

JIT: Looking forward on the path, I see a holographic gate. I will access this on my next calling and for now I stay in the TV space.

Breathes deeper

JIT: Everyone is looking at the screen which has been visually blurred so I cannot see exactly what is on there. The Orbie on the screen is speaking to those in the room. The strobes of light activate things for now and yet to come; triggers will be received on earth.

There is a beautiful sense of being, that is the only way to explain it

JIT: The inner peace and calm felt in the Orbie energy is like nothing on earth. However, it can be replicated from memory.

JIT: I can see a donkey!

JIT: I am being released.

JAN:

That was such an amazing experience. I find it so difficult to describe the out of earthly feelings, colours and connections. I felt that I was being tested as they gave me glimpses of things to come behind the opaque areas. Did you notice that I had to make a decision to continue or not? I chose to continue with this work. This could be what we see as a fork in the road of our journey. If I chose not to continue, my life would be taking a different path.

Again, not much interaction with Ques.

■ ■ ■

Jan Mayfield

Pretty Maids

09-March-2015

Present in the room

JIT: Jan in trance

Ques: Asking the questions

Reference to home is the spirit world.

Jan makes herself comfortable and begins to take herself into her altered trance state for this connection to channel their voice.

In this dialogue although there seemed to be more than one person coming through. No names were given. Therefore, all are indicated as **JIT**.

As Jan descends into her altered state, she quickly begins to speak; all the time her eyes are closed

Speaks fast, with no pauses of breath

JIT: I am taken straight into the garden.

JIT: I can hear pretty maids all in a row.

JIT: No one is with me yet. I sense lots of energy building up.

JIT: I have pressure on my head and feel like something is enveloping over me, a presence with an energy change in the room.

JIT: I can see a wonderful shade of magenta.

The first subject begins

JIT: It was on that day that Christ was born, but we don't want to go and talk about that because earth will become one again.

JIT: We will show the people of the earth. We will guide you and direct you into the places that you need to be. We will show you the way. Filters and light-force will come into force; you will be guided. Star beings are being recreated; you will feel the force, you will feel the energy, you will feel the newfound freedom.

Pause

JIT: As earth becomes one, earth also becomes two. The splits and divides will happen. They need to conquer all; the splits will happen naturally.

QUES: Earthquakes?

JIT: Higher beings. Higher beings will separate. There is no need to fear, there is no need to scurry. Just keep going about your daily lives and everything will be given to you, as it should be, when it should be. There will be divine intervention.

Voice fades

JIT: Galactical federations hold some of the keys; we hold the rest.

QUES: Who is *we*?

JIT: We work with the light; we always work with the light. Allow your light to shine.

Pause

JIT: Your light shines like a beacon.

JIT: Intergalactical we will go. We read from the books; I'll tell you the stories we see, the formulas and the creations of the past masters, the masters of the future. We see the reflection reflected to be given the answers; remember, the reflection is key.

JIT: Theories of evolution will be abandoned; theories of evolution will change. Scientific products are being soldered together, ready for the masses. Portholes and divine intervention will open up in many different areas. Look out for being connected to the ones who mirror your work in the corners of the earth.

JIT: 11 is for you.

QUES: Me or Jan, or both of us?

JIT: Jan. Later we will visit this.

Jan takes deep breaths and seems to go deeper in her altered state. The following paragraph begins in a small voice, ending with a strong and meaningful deeper voice

JIT: Daily your vibrations are changing, daily you are given new visions, new synchronicities, new thought patterns; daily this is being given. Serious and earthly transformations are taking place already; be ready, my children. Look out for the serpent, the forked tongued serpent. Look out for the fire, the fire, and the dragons that breathe the fire, the red and the orange and the yellow. Fire is breathed.

JIT: The water channels will change. The water channels will retract and detract the water channels tides. Tides reverse; the moon will change. The tides and the moon will no longer be at one. Earth's energy vibration, as it splits, will see heaven and hell on earth.

Lots of feeling and emotion in the following paragraph, rising to a raised voice with emphasis on the word Goddess

JIT: We are creating divine advancement quickly; like the speed of light the changes will occur. See from the spaceship, feel the tightening on the brow, feel the crown being placed on the heads of the royals. Goddess energy is taken forward and maybe lost in space. The Goddess energy is all around you, the

the **Goddess** energy makes space, the **Goddess** energy fuels the future, the **Goddess** energy needs to be grounded, the **Goddess** energy… is **Supreme.**

A long pause and silence

Spoken in an authoritative way as though preaching to the people

JIT: Never look under the microscope for the detail. The detail has already been created; we need to push the detail into the people and into earth. Stop looking for the minor details; it is all there, it is all at one. It has already been created, the greats began, the rest added too and now you will look at the reflection. The reflections take you to where you need to be, to where you need to go, to the things that you need to do to become one, at one with the earth as it changes as it splits.

JIT: Divine intervention will not save you; you save yourself now, you create your future now, you make way, you make the paths to take you.

Pausing and gains momentum

JIT: Logical and illogical, why try and work it out? That is not your place. Go through the time and see things change. Look at the vibrations; the room will vibrate to the highest. Feel the changes, sense the changes, and know the changes. Intergalactical I will take you. Speed up the process, come to me, speed up the process on earth, listen and do not question; feel the shifts.

JIT: Dynamite and dignitaries are placed in the borders. The borders will be no more. Peasant lands will grow, peasant lands will flourish, and peasant lands will be rewarded. Tables will turn. Stop looking for the leader; the leader is you, you are the leader. You will be guided, you will guide.

Jan breathes deep into her lungs, ready to exhale the next paragraph with vigour and authority

JIT: Abraham came to pass; everyone came to pass. Everyone came to pass; you will not come to pass.

JIT: Yours will go on forever for eternity; the great books will have written your findings my dear children. Your findings will be written in the books in the library that we show you now; your findings will be great for the future on earth. The peasant lands will understand the findings in the books.

The next line is randomly spoken in a loud, mocking voice trailing off into laughter

JIT: Dog eared Chiwowa, what does that mean, Chiwowwwa wwwwwa?

Quickly moves on to say

JIT: Medicine is in your hands, in your being, in your thoughts, in your eyes, in your vision; that is where the medicines are.

JIT: Be at one with nature; be at one with self, be at one. See the whole. See the whole open up in front of you, see the whole. Mind numbing games and creation (*tut*) throw them in the bin I say. Be at one, tardiced and recluse, be at one.

Gently spoken

JIT: Happy and in love, love holds the key.

Pausing now and rhythmically spoken

JIT: Look at the Scottish, the Scots have it, look at the Scots, they have it. Visit the Scottish and take the opportunities to visit the Scottish.

JIT: You will be placed there.

JIT: You will be placed in America.

JIT: You will be placed in Canada.

JIT: You will be placed in the Scottish.

JIT: You will have rest periods.

Long pause here, deep breaths being taken and the voice changes to a more meaningful, deeper searching...

JIT: There are vibrations open; so are the channels of love and guidance. As the vibrations become higher pathways for the earthlings, they will pick up the seeds of love as they travel along these vibrations. Just as you two have done, my children.

JIT: You have guided, **you** have sown the seeds to enable them to jump into the vibrations and move in interconnecting ways. We will lift you out now. We will lift you out and continue you on your journey of discoveries and reaching.

A short pause

JIT: Concluding, you will reach and conclude with divine guidance, divine intervention. With a little scientific mumbo jumbo *(said with humour)*. The conclusion is here. The conclusion we will give you when the time is right.

JIT: My children, today as this chapter draws to a close, know that you are being guided. Have been guided; have been given information from the highest of the highest. I leave you now to rise in your vibrations and I leave you now to complete today, to the date tomorrow great things will happen.

JIT: 10 3 15 great things will happen, feel the shift and the change as you walk forward; know that you are being guided, loved and challenged.

JIT: Information will be downloaded directly from the source to the earthling you call *Jan*.

JIT: This information she will receive over the coming 7 weeks. You must inform her to keep a log and journal of specific points, names, and values. She will understand. We have done this before; we have tested. She has done this before and she retrieves it well.

JIT: I will return; I will return for the final chapter of our writing works together. I will return.

Softer voice

JIT: Questions

QUES: What is my role?

JIT: Support

QUES: Is this book coming to the conclusion then?

JIT: One more chapter, my friend, I will return.

QUES: Is there anything we or I need to know?

JIT: Listen, hear, see and take in. Make notes and process information that is given to you to help you in your personal life. You will sit with Jan until the last trance is delivered.

QUES: What is my spirit name?

JIT: Umbilical.

JIT: Umbilical and I have to say this is an important name.

JIT: Can see a flower in the belly button of Ques with a stalk and it all opens up to bloom in the most enchanting way.

JIT: Any more questions?

QUES: No.

JAN:

I felt this session to be a very important one with an abundance of information and confirmations to life. Maybe you will need to read it twice. As I transcribed, I had a sense of sadness towards the end as there were so many questions that could have been asked. The opportunity was given and not taken, as with many things in life, we choose. And Ques chose not to ask any more questions.

Ques does not see the significance of her spirit name. I am told not to say anymore as she will have to work through this herself in her own time. It is very significant to her present life.

The channellings close on this chapter.

■ ■ ■

Chapter 6

AS ONE CHAPTER CLOSES, ANOTHER DOOR OPENS
My Life Experiences Continue

∞ ∞ ∞

As One Chapter Closes, Another Door Opens

'Ques' faded away as the last chapter of recordings were completed; she had other things to do in life. I missed the connection to the trance sessions, but knew it was all for the greater good. In this chapter, you will read some of my experiences as a medium. Knowing that the writing is paused and I must continue with challenges as they present themselves.

My life is never short of spiritual experiences. I am happy and totally believe and have the faith that progression is for the greater good of this life's journey.

Many times I would open my laptop to begin typing and there was nothing. There were no words to create a follow up chapter.

Would you like to be on a show? This was the first sentence in an email I opened from a TV company in Europe. I knew deep inside that I had to do this, but I was not sure of the reasons behind it. I am often guided to do things in my life that turn out to be totally different than the original intentions.

I agreed, but cannot comment too much about the programme. I am going to say that there were so many people working from ego and wanted fame. I did not want either. My reason to be there would be to show the world what we do as a psychic/medium is 'real'.

I was concerned as to why I was guided there, as I learned that this would not be how we would be portrayed. We talk about free-will to choose when opportunities present themselves. I chose to go.

I said a little prayer to spirit and asked them to allow me not to go any further forward if it was not the intention. I asked them to only give me the experiences that I needed.

A few days later after a location setting, we had to perform a little test.

Two set members came into my room with two photographs for me to read. This is something I do often and have done for many years.

When I looked at the pictures I had nothing in my head, spirits were in the room but not talking to me! After a conversation in my head, saying that I trust them but please give me something, information flooded into my head but not the two specifics they were looking for.

I then asked spirit why I was on the show if it was not to take part.

To meet with egos

To meet with those who seek fame

To be true to myself and my work

To see the real reason for being there

To visit that beautiful country

I knew I was not meant to go any further.

I made friends with one who wanted fame... there lies another story! There was another person who I was to share a reading session with.

My hotel room was adorned with gold fabric, deeply embossed wallpaper and sparse furniture surrounding the four-poster bed. In one corner was an ornate round glass topped side table. I had picked up so many energies in that room from the moment that I walked in, my confirmation to be there.

In the day, I chatted with a lovely man who worked in the paranormal field but had never had a close connection with a Medium like me. He asked if he could have a private sitting.

He came along to my room and we sat at the round table, I began the reading and connected to someone who had not long passed. He looked at me but he could not speak in amazement, at the words I had for him.

His native tongue was not English and he wanted to ask questions to this spirit. I told him to ask in his own language. He asked the questions and the spirits gave me the answers which I could explain to him. He was crying with release and relief, knowing that his friend was safe. The whole room filled with love a spirit energies.

That was another reason to be there. It was such a beautiful experience to share. I stayed for ten days in all. Returning to a little retreat I use to do my writing.

Lifting the lid of my laptop with the intention to continue writing this book, the words still did not come, emptiness and silence was all I had. Distracting myself, I began reading emails and generally perusing the internet.

A friend who visits the area where my writing retreat is, shared a link to a missing person in her home town through a social media network. As I read this, I felt emotional for the person and their family. Periodically, I am asked to work on missing person's cases but I have never felt such a strong connection as this. As hard as I tried to get on with my day, I kept coming back to this one. My head was full of information about the situation. I knew I could not ignore it.

I decided to give the spirits permission to connect me and I found myself sketching a map of an area I knew absolutely nothing about.

I could see the places this person had been the night they went missing and the route that was walked. There were so many other details too.

This information was so strong I knew it had to be passed on, so I sent a message to my friend with the copy of my drawing and all that had come through from spirit. This put her on the spot a little, as she now needed to decide if she should take it further. Her friend also confirmed the sketch was exactly like the area of one of the sightings. The information was given to the police.

In the meantime, I had arranged a visit to her hometown; I had never been to that area of the United Kingdom and was excited to be going. I thought the missing person would have been found before my travel date.

He was still missing and I was travelling that day with a 4.5hr flight and a train journey, which took me to the Highlands where my friend joined me at the station. I was happy and excited to see her. I was also in a state of anticipation. She began to drive me around the area that I had seen in my mind's eye.

Waves of strong feelings came over me, with déjà vu moments. I knew where I was and where I wanted to go. I spoke of how I felt as we drove around and she informed me of what she knew of the area.

I then needed to go to a particular green on a golf course overlooking the sea, as I had seen the rocks in the water in my mind's eye. She told me there were no rocks and the area had been searched many times since the disappearance.

We arrived in the area and I told her where to stop the car; I knew exactly where I was going. I walked a little ahead, as my steps were faster. I was like a hunting dog with the scent, but the scent was in my mind. I knew the exact path that had been trodden. The long grass and the short manicured green all had an invisible path, but not to my eye. I was him. I was his energy and I knew the way he had walked, where he had stumbled and where he had sat. My heart was beating fast. My friend stood back and never once interrupted me. She knew of my work and we have a wonderful friendship that goes beyond knowing.

I was very emotional, upset and disorientated; these were the energies of the missing person. I shouted to my friend to show her the rocks; they were exactly where I said they were. Previous searches had not revealed the rocks as the tide was higher and they were covered in the salty sea water. I became emotional and breathless to the point of gasping. We stayed for a while as I walked along the shore to satisfy my mind of my visions.

I knew I had to make a statement to the police, if nothing else than to clear it out of my mind, and there may have been a little piece of evidence that was needed. We went to the local police station and I gave a statement the day before I left. This police station was connected to the one in the small town where he was from and where the original information from me was given. But this police station knew nothing about it. I never heard anything from the police. It seems there is no central way of communicating! Is this the 21st century?

Deep inside, I sensed he might not be found alive, but in all these cases you hang on to a little something that you may be wrong. It was a day later that he was pronounced deceased. He had been taken by the undercurrents and tides, the newspaper said. I know he entered the water at the

the point of the rocks, there is no proof, it is all in my head!

I spent time with my friend and her husband and she introduced me to The Highlands!

I was then to give readings at someone's house. The readings were great and it was lovely to meet some wonderful people. The son of the family whose house I was at wanted to take part, but was unsure so we suggested he just listen. His great grandfather was there to deliver a message to him that would be the message that began to change his life for the better.

It is so amazing how messages from the other side can encourage us to make changes in our present lives. The connection and the belief that life goes on, seems to give validation that we are looked after.

Over the years, I have witnessed many life-changing experiences for those who connect with me.

After some sightseeing and visits to castles, churches and lots of blethering (chatting) with my friend, it was time for me to leave. I gathered my life experiences and continued on my journey.

As the train sped through the glens and stopped at the unfamiliar stations, I wondered what was in store for me and why I had been taken off my writing. My mind wandered and was given this verse by Isaac, Grannie Mary's brother.

■ ■ ■

Past To Present

God's water transcends, over valleys and glens.

Lush greens and the luck of the purple heather.

Listen as you hear the words unsaid.

The language of the inhabitants' highs and lows, dulcet tones.

Expanses of water meeting tides, swells and exposure.

Open structure anchored gathering water's resources.

The whirring, the swirling, the elegant and white, more of nature's intended.

Dolphins and seals, northern lights, isles, land points and shores.

Capture, envelop and desire, what man cannot endure.

The highlands, the lowlands the perfection reflected for all to see.

Look beyond to gasp with pleasured memories.

■ ■ ■

I relaxed with my thoughts and the polite conversation from the gentleman who sat opposite. It wasn't long before I had sensations from spirits to let me know they are around. Usually this is a time when they want me to connect to someone and give a message. I do not randomly go up to people in the street and give messages. However, if a conversation goes that way, I will.

Just like the time I was a passenger on an aircraft with a 4-hour journey ahead, I always choose the window seat. On this flight there was a free seat between me and the person on the aisle seat. We said hello; he was dressed in a pilot's uniform and not very old. He was very proud of being a pilot and was heading for his next assignment. We relaxed as we sampled the complementary meal and drinks. We chatted on and off. It was about one hour into the journey when the spirits started talking to me.

Tell him I am here, go on tell him.

Oh my, this was so strong, but how could I tell someone on a plane that their grandfather was with me? How? This young pilot had no escape route!

Anyway, we chatted some more and I was telling the grandfather spirit in my head that if he had a message then he must build it into the conversation for me. He kept showing me music and a grand piano he loved to play. He told me how much he loved his grandson and was proud of his achievements, and he wanted him to know that he was looking after him.

True to form, they did not let me down. The pilot began talking about families, so I mentioned my grandma and he mentioned his grandfather; I was able to say *I bet he liked music*. He just looked at me quizzically but said *yes he did*. I said I could imagine him playing the piano, and there was a piece of music that always reminded him of his grandfather... Again, he looked, but I felt comfortable to carry on.

There were some more exchanges and eventually I said that I often sense my grandma from her perfume, and he said that whenever he thinks of his grandfather he hears music. I went on to say how proud grandparents are of their grandchildren. A couple of other things that he said made me realise that his grandfather was somehow giving him thoughts, as his words were the same as the visions I was given.

So as you can see, there are many ways to get a message to someone. We didn't speak much for the rest of the journey. But when we parted he shook my hand and said thank you. I knew his grandfather's eyes were looking at me through him. I smiled and felt so humbled.

The train was still speeding through the countryside. Eventually, I arrived at my destination and catching up with family and friends would take up my time for a while now.

I had many readings/demonstrations and private spiritual parties booked for the coming months. An evening was booked on a ghost hunt paranormal event which turned out to be different. Our experiences at this event can be read on my website. It's called, *Ghost Hunting From A Medium's Point of View.*

The following weeks came and went as I worked in and around the UK.

A lady contacted me to go to her house and read for her; I have been seeing her for about 3 years following the death of her husband. I watched as she came to terms with his death and saw her ongoing struggle to be living without the person she loved dearly.

This lady is amazing and she takes every word that her husband gives her to help her personal grieving process. He has given so much over the years and at my last visit, I sat with her and we worked through how to sense him around. She wanted to so much, but had been unable to really sense his energy. We sat together and I asked him to come close and show her how he would let her know he was around. It was another amazing experience for all of us. She felt him/energy, and she now knows his signs and feels comfortable with this.

I wondered what we would talk about on this visit. I began to sense his energy as I drove past the church where his grave is situated. His spirit stayed with me in the car and talked a little. I knocked on her door and as she opened it she looked radiant; with a big smile on her face she was happy to see me and of course her husband (whom she didn't see), who was pushing in front of me.

I sat in my usual seat on the brown leather sofa, my bag on my lap and my notebook on top of that, with a poised pen to make notes for her to keep as a reminder of the things we say. *(As I type this I have a déjà vu moment, and look back over the chapters as I remember one of the trance sessions mentioning brown leather, it was in Black Dot. Maybe it was referring to this sofa.)*

I asked how she had been getting on and she was so pleased that she had the confidence to sense his energy, and recognise his presence.

I began to pass on words from him and he guided us to talk about his time in hospital, especially the days and hours before he passed. I know that these were traumatic times as there had been a lot of problems with doctors/consultants and miscommunication.

I was guided by her husband to put my notebook down and listen to him; he was to take me through those times in my mind's eye. Remember, I see everything that the person is showing me, either as a film or through their eyes, and that feels like a memory. I was becoming him and seeing through his eyes. I double checked that she was sure she wanted me to do this. We trusted that he would give us what she needed to hear.

I became him. As I lay in the hospital bed I was shown the ceiling, the monitors, wires and drips to the left and a chair; to the right of the bed I was shown his wife sitting on a chair looking at me/him. I could see a doctor entering the room and looking at me, then looking at the monitors, but not at my wife. I saw she was very sad but she had no tears. That doctor went and another one came in. I felt as though my chest was tight and my eyes were starting to see familiar people in the room. I was floating and lifting and feeling rather enigmatic.

Wow... I missed all that and saw the ceiling again, and doctors around the bed... I had been shocked.

I wanted to go back to the familiar faces. I did and as I was moved out of my earthly body. I had this wonderful sense of peace and knowing that I was going to the right place. I was moving through to another dimension and was greeted by familiar people. We walked and moved to the place I needed to be. I was taken to see someone, a welcoming sphere who sat next to; he directed my vision to a screen. We sat and watched together. It was my life on earth that was shown to me, from birth to moving through to this dimension. There were so many wonderful, out-of-earthly colours and senses that are difficult to explain in earthly words as there just aren't the words.

I let his soul go, and spoke as Jan. I relayed how I flowed across and how beautiful everything was, and how peaceful I felt moving through, transitioning.

There was more information I gave which was personal to them, and she had questions surrounding is death answered.

I felt so highly honoured to have been given this experience in a reading, to travel the path to the "other side". I really was in awe of what I was able to do for the greater good of this lady.

I have travelled through death before, but not in such a detailed way and not with the communication between husband and wife. Thank you.

Many people have regression in hypnosis with a bid to heal themselves from the past; I had it to see what I had been in past lives and how those lives influenced this one.

I have a trusted friend who is a hypnotherapist and he was talking about progression, which is going forward in your own life, and the chance to go through death. I was very interested in this and asked for him to take me there. All I will say is that I was taken through my own death and it was an experience that I am so pleased I had. This happened about 6 years ago and it is a memory for me now, one that one day I will experience.

I have my beliefs, experiences as a medium, dreams and visions that I am given in meditation and trance sessions. I know and believe there is more to life than what we experience on earth.

This chapter has given you a glimpse into the life of a medium and also shown you how recognising why you are in a particular situation can often give you clarity and avoid years of anguish and heartache.

I knew that the next chapter would begin with trances going through death; I had the voices in my head telling me and they kept referring to the last reading I had done. That was my introduction to the following chapter.

I wondered who would sit with me, as I had only heard from Ques briefly in the time that I was gathering my life experiences.

■ ■ ■

Jan Mayfield

<u>Chapter 7</u>

TRANCING LIFE'S UNIVERSAL ENERGIES

∞ ∞ ∞

Introduction To Trancing Life's Universal Energies

Life has brought me back to my writing retreat and in contact again with Ques. Although she is not in a good place within herself, she has agreed to be in the room whilst I trance.

All I know at the beginning of this chapter, is that the following dialogues will lead on from the reading which I gave a few weeks' prior, moving through death. This is informative and not in the slightest morbid.

These dialogues, like the suicide ones, evolve. I do not want to influence your thoughts; please read with an open mind and visualise the descriptions from each voiced soul.

As I transcribe, I am transported into the trance session. I am reliving the emotions, personality, sensations and visions of the voice. It feels like I have experienced their passing; somehow I am lost in time as I type and it all becomes a memory.

George continues to appear from nowhere as in some of the previous trances.

The sessions have been grouped as the energies altered.

■ ■ ■

Sessions 1-3

Transitioning from all perspectives.

Continuing from the last chapter with the passing through to the spirit world, we are now given a glimpse into the greater universe and what becomes of the soul as it transitions. Information from Orbies and the transitioned soul's perspective.

These sessions give guidance on your choices in Pre-A and how they are shown to you on screen for evaluation.

01 Trance

23-Jan-2016

Present in the room

JIT: Jan in trance

Ques: Asking the questions

Jan makes herself comfortable and begins to take herself into her altered trance state for this connection to channel their voice.

Jan feels a tightness around her head as the spirits come into the room. Their energies fill her personal space.

Spoken slowly in the opening dialogue

JIT: I can feel, I sense a car, I can see a car. I know I am in a car, a black car, I am driving.

There is a pause here and a feeling of mixed emotions and hesitation

JIT: I am hit by a lorry; I can see a lorry. My legs are trapped.

There is a long pause

There is a sense of sadness in the voice

JIT: I am the driver. I know I am that person and I know I am talking.

JIT: I am in the car and I can feel my legs are trapped and my body forced back. I passed out.

There is so much emotion in this for Jan as she speaks as the driver

JIT: I am the person who passed out.

More spirits are around, making a stronger connection

JIT: I look up inside my eyes which is their vision.

JIT: I can see flashes and I can see faces. The faces belong to the person in the car. (The driver)

The faces are people who have already passed over

JIT: I can see a boy on a scooter.

JIT: I can see a grandma and granddad's face. I can see the name Josie. I can see France -the word not the place.

People who have passed are visiting him

JIT: All of this is going on in front of my eyes. All have passed over before.

JIT: I am also aware there was someone sitting in the car next to me who isn't there now.

JIT: I am also aware of someone putting their fingers on my neck.

Jan points to her neck

There are vibrations in the car and so much noise

JIT: The car is cut open by the fire brigade. I am lifted out.

JIT: I can see people and faces; we are looking at spirit people here.

JIT: Ambulance. I don't think my heart is beating. I am not in the body in the ambulance. I am looking down at the ambulance. I have left my earthly body.

Jan experiences the sensations of resuscitation

And becomes breathless and irritated as she trances the voice

JIT: I can feel my chest being pressed and I am shocked by the machine that restarts your heart.

JIT: I can see a cord from the ambulance to the person looking into the ambulance (soul). It is still attached to the ambulance.

Soul returns to their earthly body

JIT: I am inside the ambulance I am... (Has gone back into the body) I see someone looking at me, a male face, and a doctor.

JIT: I have a sense that the ambulance is moving; they are driving fast. I can hear the siren and see flashes of the blue light.

JIT: I can see the people in the ambulance looking at each other. Just looking. I don't understand. They are looking at my chest and holding my wrists then they look at machines.

JIT: I feel sick.

JIT: I am being taken out of the ambulance and being rushed into the cubicle.

Jan's head is tighter with more spirits around

JIT: Everything is rushed.

Someone shouts

JIT: Cubicle!

JIT: I can't feel my legs, I have no sensations or feelings, and I don't seem to be worried about this.

JIT: The trolley bed is taken out of there to somewhere else.

JIT: There is so much urgency as everyone is running to get me to the lift.

JIT: I can't swallow; there are machines.

JIT: I... I... I can still see the faces and they make me happy.

JIT: Machines. I can see all the machines attached to my body.

JIT is breathless as she speaks

JIT: A lady looks at me and cries; she is shocked. Her hand is over her mouth! I can see the people now...the faces... spirit faces.

In and out of consciousness, goes from people in the room to the faces in the mind.

Spoken slowly

JIT: I don't know what they are doing, pushing and touching my body, poking and prodding.

JIT: My mind, pushing a tube in my side, pushing it in. They haven't got time for something.

JIT: The lady is crying as she looks at me.

JIT: I see a little girl; she pops in and is ushered out by the lady.

There is a pause

Faces appear, all around

The speech is slower

JIT: I can see faces again. I see my grandma. I see my granddad and I see a little baby. I see someone walking down the road.

JIT: There are lots of lights, like orbs but bright and as they come towards me, they change into faces that I recognise from my life before.

He states

JIT: Not bodies, just faces.

JIT: I take a look behind me and the lady is crying.

Mumbles of the faces talking, but not speaking to each other and they know what they are saying… telepathy?

JIT: I have a look at the circle who is Grandma and I know all the faces. She changes too.

Past lives or relatives?

JIT: Sometimes the faces are young, some old, the faces change and show me.

JIT: I just know it is right.

A sense that he has the knowing feeling of being in the right place

Speaking very intensely and slowly

JIT: All is black, dark, but we can see each other. The faces go; the circles just shine and come back, looking at me to see if I am still there.

JIT: I can see faces behind me and in front of me; they are showing me the way as everywhere is black. I am guided by the lights in the circles when they are not faces.

More about faces

JIT: The faces come closer and I can see pink, turquoise and orange.

A pause, while JIT takes in what is happening

JIT: I am in a place just appeared, like a room; it is just a space.

You can feel the sense of being overwhelmed in her voice, very emotional

JIT: Full of such beauty, I have overwhelming recognition, overwhelming everything.

Very softly spoken, almost like a voice before sleep, very relaxed and gentle

JIT: I don't see the faces now; I see the circles that are like balls. (Orbs)

JIT: There are so many of them and they all seem to be doing something, but I can't see what they are doing.

JIT: It is just a knowing. They are very busy, animated but still.

Jan is waiting to see where they go now; there are feelings but no visuals in the black

JIT: Three green ones are coming towards me; we go 'round a corner and down in the black like it is just space. I feel like I am turning and as I look forward it opens up again. (*Opens up into what could be a room.*)

JIT: They are showing me… They are talking; I can't hear them but I know they are talking.

JIT: Communicating.

Voice is so quiet and focused

JIT: In earth on earth there were 3. I see a screen with lines going through it. Each line has a year of age on it.

JIT: I can see 3 years old. Someone talks to me about 3YO, 11YO, 17YO and 22YO; he talks to me about these times. My life is discussed and these are important points.

22YO, 28YO, it is showing me different things at 28YO.

Very soft voice

JIT: I did it wrong at 28; I did it wrong. At 31 there is nothing else. 31 and I am here.

Am I this age when I passed?

JIT: I am being taken back to 28YO; the screen is showing me 28. At this age there were 3 different roads/lines.

JIT: One line was the same as my life before.

JIT: Another line/life path; I could not go down that one because I was not strong and I listened to other people. They took me to places and showed me things and gave me excitement. I thought they were special.

JIT: The other line/life path, I can see the woman and children; I see it as happy and helping. It is one, long line/life path. I went down that one and I couldn't see. I was led by the people and I can see people arguing with the lady. I shouted; I wasn't very nice to her.

These are his life lines

The following is said very slowly in short sentences

JIT: I went out in the car.

JIT: I was angry.

JIT: I was driving along.

JIT: I was looking at her and shouting.

JIT: She was looking at me and crying.

JIT: Carried on along the road, I was driving fast.

JIT: She was looking at me.

JIT: There is a lorry coming out from the side road smashing into the car.

JIT: The person shows me that is why I am here.

Choice

JAN: Free-will to choose that path?

JIT: I hadn't learned my lesson from before because I could not say *no*. If I had taken the other path it went on for longer.

JIT: Showing me the other path now.

JIT: It still ends in the same way; I am in the car and a lorry collides with it. In this path there is no lady on the side of me in the car.

JIT: I am alone.

Goes back to childhood

Spoken in the same tone, slow and methodical with emotion

JIT: I was 5 and my grandparents bought me a black toy car and a lorry. I used to play with the cars and the lorry; I used to make them crash.

JIT: I never had an ambulance (*said sadly*)

The screen is turned off

JIT: I continue past that screen room and the green circles/orbs come and show me where to go. They take me.

Voice picks up speed and volume

JIT: I am with some other orbs; they are all the same colour. We talk to each other but don't speak. We hear each other.

JIT: Lots of screens around the space; no walls.

JIT: I can see earth. We can zoom in on earth. There are different planets on another screen.

JIT: Another screen is a library full of books, but it is not earthly. You can go in that screen and have a look at the books anytime.

JIT: I just know I should be...

JAN:

This session gave insight into all elements of passing and how life choices can affect our lives.

Do we always see the choices?

In the transition of passing from the earthly body to the spirit world, we were given first hand insight as transition takes place. I have a sense of contentment as I transcribe this session.

Many people feel stuck in their life and will book a private session with me. In this session, I have the skill to know when they have experienced traumatic events going back to birth. They will then know what their subconscious is holding onto, enabling them to release. We can access past life events in the same way.

Exactly as given in this dialogue. It is a skill I have been given to help people move on to living their soul's purpose.

This enables them to work on releasing the events, heal from the past to enable the true future.

■ ■ ■

02 Trance

23-Jan-2016

Present in the room

JIT: Jan in trance

JAN: Jan as Jan

Ques: Asking the questions

Jan makes herself comfortable and begins to take herself into her altered trance state for this connection to channel their voice.

JAN: My first vision is of kangaroos; and an intense emotional feeling of sadness but with a beautiful warmth all over my body.

Breathes deeply

Exhales deeper into trance

JAN: I remember, as I was going into the altered state, that I could see so many faces and pictures flashing in front of my eyes, and some were very disturbing… blood on their bodies and horrific facial expressions.

Speaking in trance

JIT: I have a feeling of happiness and freedom.

JIT: I hear the words. *I have escaped*. I hear the word *trauma.*

JIT: I am floating above something, looking down.

Very deep breathing until a deep state has been reached

JIT: There is too much going on to see clearly.

JIT: I see a big tent with beds on either side of the tent inside. It is a hospital tent.

A feeling of confusion

JIT: Blood, there is lots of blood. I don't know where I am...

Sounds very lost and disorientated

Ques: Is it your blood?

So slow is the voice and almost slurred from emotion

Says the words below with no constructed sentences

He seems too tired to put more words together

JIT: Everybody's blood.

JIT: There are people on the beds.

JIT: Bandages.

JIT: Crying, shouting, silence.

Jan is a little agitated

JIT: Bottles of water to wash the blood, washing the bodies. Bandages are on their head, legs and some on their eyes.

Such sadness

JIT: Some haven't got legs now.

Realisation… sadness

JIT: Looking for mine. I can't find mine. Where are mine?

JIT: Looking along all the beds, looking along all sides.

JIT: Some people are in bags. I can't see their faces; 40 plus people. There must be.

There is so much emotion in the words spoken

JIT: I can hear bangs, loud bangs; the sound vibrates through the air and causes pain in my ears.

JIT: I am coming out of the hospital tent; I am looking for me, looking for myself.

This is in slow motion

JIT: Coming out of the tent, so many people shouting and crying, holding the bodies. There are so many bodies.

JIT: Looking at the bags.

JIT: Moves on to another tent.

JIT: A massive tent.

JIT: It was just bags with bodies in.. all along the side of the tent.

JIT: Must be a mortuary.

Slowly spoken

Breathes deep

JIT: Bags with numbers on.

Jan agitated

JIT: I am looking at all the bags slowly.

JIT: I don't understand what they are saying... Different language.. not English.

JIT: I can't see and I am not in the bags.

JIT: Coming out of that tent. I am not there.

Desperately looking for his body

JIT: I want to find my body. Where is my body?

JIT: Going into another tent.

JIT: Going into another tent.

Makes a disgusted noise

States what can be seen

JIT: Bodies on the floor, not in a bag, have a sheet over.

JIT: I have found mine.

Spoken slowly

JIT: I know that is me.

JIT: I know that is me.

JIT: I go back in that body and I want to have a look.

JIT: I go back in... (*soul enters body*)

JIT: Move my arms.

JIT: People come running over.

JIT: Take the cover off my face.

JIT: See my arms move then...

JIT: I look up at their faces. They can't hide the horror; they can't hide their devastation.

JIT: They are tired. They are hungry. They are working so hard.

JIT: Look at my body moving.

Jan has a sick feeling in her stomach

JIT: I come back out again now and I watch from above... soul leaves the body again.

JIT: They roll me over. Into the bag now for my body.

JIT: Clearly decapitated.

JIT: I let them. I watch them put me in the bag.

JIT: I come away from the smell and devastation and trauma.

JIT: The smell.

The smell.

The smell... (*Said slowly with big sighs*)

JIT: It is like I am being pulled after I was released from the body.

JIT: And I am being pulled now.

JIT: It is like there is a magnet pulling me; I have no control and am just going. I am being pulled very fast and strong.

Slow speech with a little more depth as he travels into transition

JIT: Very strong. It feels good. It feels right. Being pulled. Nowhere, I can't see. Just pulled and pulled.

JIT: I can see circles and faces. I can see some balls. I go past them all.

Keep going...

Keep going...

JIT: I can see stables of orbs. So many. All different colours. All the same colours together, none of the colours are mixed.

I keep going...

JIT: I can't see my body or anything; I am in the black being pulled and it is like I am on a roller coaster but there is no roller coaster.

JIT: I stop now.

And wait

JIT: Still on my own.

JIT: I don't sense.

JIT: It's like I am just hanging there suspended in the black.

JIT: A screen is popping up in front of me. Whatever they are wanting to show me is being rewound.

JIT: Everything on the screen is going backwards.

JIT: I can see the hospital tent.

JIT: I can see the bodies.

JIT: I can see the bodies without limbs.

JIT: It is all going backwards on the screen.

JIT: Back, back, back.

JIT: It does not want to stop rewinding.

Here is his story of life on earth, on the screen

The voice is a little brighter with slow speech

Speak of what is on the screen

JIT: I was born on earth.

JIT: A baby. Mother is sad. And happy. She loves me so much.

JIT: I start to grow to a child. And a man comes into my life. I look at him; I know him; I recognise him as my father. I don't remember him from before. They showed me a picture on the television. It is the same face.

JIT: This is your father, just black and white.

JIT: The television is small.

JIT: There was an open fire with not much coal on it. Goes away again… the father.

JIT: Love my mum and my grandma, my auntie.

Pause

Monotone voice

JIT: Go to school. The boys at school.

JIT: I go home one day my mum is crying. Auntie is crying. Grandma is crying.

JIT: Father is gone; they tell me my father is gone.

JIT: I didn't understand, he has gone before and they did not cry.

JIT: Now he is **gone.**

JIT: Everybody cries for a long time.

Pauses

JIT: I can hear sirens and screeching, bomb noises, blasts; everybody hides.

JIT: I am walking down the road with a gun. I am now in my uniform and I am so proud. I can see Mum, Auntie and Grandma.

JIT: They say I am just like my father.

JIT: I go. They cry. I go.

JIT: I walk down the street.

JIT: People on the doorsteps waving.

JIT: I go to where everyone else is; all dressed the same and have guns.

JIT: The shelter.

JIT: I go on a boat.

Voice becomes quiet again

JIT: The screen shows me sand on the floor and mountains not too far in the distance. The screen shows me people crouching down with the guns pointing at an area I can't see.

JIT: The screen shows me fighting.

JIT: And starting.

JIT: The screen shows me people being shot. Chest, arms. Chest.

JIT: The screen shows me them falling into the holes.

JIT: Ugh, devastated.

JIT: The screen shows me people running forward. Big blast throwing them into the air... people then fall to the ground.

JIT: The screen then shows me standing up, looking forward.

JIT: Ugh.

Very slowly speaks each word with a pause at the end of each line

JIT: My neck feels warm...

JIT: I drop my gun...

JIT: My knees bend...

JIT: I feel my face going white, pale and cold... I fall to the ground.

JIT: I can see that from the screen but somehow I know what it feels like.

JIT: Just before my neck feels warm, the tie was cut from the body. I watched everything.

JIT: I watched from a distance.

JIT: I watched it all with meaningless. Just meaningless.

Breathes

JIT: I wanted to go back and see what it was like so I went back in when I was in the tent. *(In his body)*

JIT: It shook a bit as he went in.

JIT: I saw the people coming over when my body shook.

JIT: It was not my place anymore.

JIT: I came out again.

JIT: The screen is closing now.

Pausing for a while

JIT: I am being pulled somewhere else away from the screen.

JIT: I get shown a room but it has no walls or floor; it is like a hologram.

JIT: I can go into the room.

JIT: I know that in this room, I can ask to be asked to taken to any part of my life as I have lived before. On earth or planets as human or animal or plant I can revisit at any time.

JIT: For now, I am just being shown it.

JIT: I am being pulled further now.

JIT: Feels like I am going up but I don't know. It is just space. If I look to the right of me I can see what looks like earth. My eyes can be taken right down to earth; I can pinpoint at any given time where I am needed. I carry on now. I don't want to go there.

The voice is a little faster

JIT: I see 4 orbs sitting, standing, and hovering.

JIT: I am not dragged. Now I am with them. 5 of us.

JIT: I have to help the other orbs; I turn around to show the way.

JIT: I will never return to earth.

JIT: I will visit planets when the time is right.

JIT: I will revisit.

■ ■ ■

With a different voice Jan stays in trance and states the following.

JIT: The time is coming now to help the children, the children born of the 80s and 90s. They will need the help as earth evolves; so will the people.

JIT: The people on earth have been selected to enable others.

JIT: Congeal with substances never seen before. Life on earth will change. Earth will change.

JIT: 2027 will show a great big spin, a spin of destruction, a spin of maturity, a spin of releasing. Those children will then be the ones to lead and take forward earthly life, **not** as you know it today.

JIT: 2031 will show things decomposing. They will show combustion of inanimate objects. They will show robotics necessary to act out earthly things without emotion.

JIT: 2032 will join the states and eliminate those who no longer conduct themselves for the love of life on earth. Mother Nature will rebel; Mother Nature will take you into the sea down beyond any sea that has been visited in recent years; there will be doors opening up below for people.

JIT: You will revisit the Aquarius.

JIT: People will walk below the pyramids, not in or up; people will walk below.

JIT: The earth will quake; the sand will open to reveal the mirror image of the pyramids below what we see now; many temples will be rebuilt.

JIT: Many earthquakes will break to reveal the images below.

Spoken in a meaningful way, almost as if being read

JIT: There will be no fighting.

JIT: There will be no disobedience.

JIT: There will be harmony on earth.

JIT: Those who choose not to harmonise will not see what is below.

JIT: They will be taken to the places that we are showing you now.

JIT: The sky will align with certain areas on earth. Stars will produce strength in energy when connected to the earth; they will send down light to pierce the earth. Now is the time to prepare the children for those times ahead.

JIT: Those who are not prepared will fall off the earth; they will fall by the wayside.

JIT: The American states will merge and morph into one land.

JIT: 19... 72

JAN:

As I type the dialogue, I am taken in my mind to the trance which is so horrifically disturbing. I shed tears as I type. Clearly, the soul was looking for their earthly body to be reunited. However, as the soul re-entered the body and the medics rushed to help, there would be no unity as the human body had been decapitated.

The soul was released again. I do not know where this was or how many years ago. Seeing such devastation from this point of view and to become a "happy" soul, indicates that all earthly emotions are shed in the transition, continuing our eternal life.

The second part of the trance session seemingly revealed what look like some predictions for our future on earth.

■ ■ ■

03 Trance

25-Feb-2015

Present in the room

JIT: Jan in trance

JAN: Jan as Jan

Ques: Asking the questions

Jan makes herself comfortable and begins to take herself into her altered trance state for this connection to channel their voice.

Jan came straight in with these words

JIT: Beyond the grave, Margaretta.

JIT: Hello.

Ques: Hello.

JIT: Can you see me?

Ques: No, I can't see you, but I can hear you.

Inquisitively

JIT: What are all those people doing looking in the hole?

Ques: Are you in the hole?

JIT: I am looking at the people looking into the hole.

Ques: Is it a funeral?

JIT: All crying.

Ques: Do you want to talk to me?

JIT: Just watching.

Ques: Are you just watching?

Ques: Are you Margaretta?

JIT: No.

Ques: Who is Margaretta?

JIT: In the hole.

Ques: Who are you?

JIT: Everyone.

Ques: Are you waiting for Margaretta?

JIT: Going backwards now.

JIT: Going backwards.

JIT: Being pulled backwards.

JIT: Back, going back. Into the black. Into the screen now.

Pause

JIT: I can see the hole in the screen. The screen is going backwards; the film on the screen is going backwards.

Ques: Are you watching Margaretta?

Ignored that question

JIT: Three children I had.

JIT: Three children all grown up into beautiful girls.

JIT: I brought them up on my own. They have their lives but I still want to be part of it.

JIT: The screen shows me this, the screen shows me one child is ill. In and out of hospital lots of times with that one. Sometimes I used to think my life would be easier without the visits to the hospital.

JIT: Just like a thorn in my side. I loved her but felt restricted, which I was.

JIT: I loved unconditionally too that daughter and the others.

JIT: 19, 20, 21, 22, 23, 24, 25 (*she counts*) she was 25 and did not have to go to hospital anymore; she was fine.

JIT: 39 40 41 42 43 44 45 49 59 62 72 82 62 52 85 82 89 82 89 82… 82 I am. Why did it stop on 82?

JIT: I was not balanced at 82.

JIT: The scales were weighing heavy on the left side. Doom and gloom on the left side.

JIT: The thorn in my side was causing problems; more problems were created.

JIT: Everything in the world looks fine; I cannot speak. My mouth opens but the words do not come out.

JIT: I can't speak. I can't feel my body on my left hand side. I can't walk. I can't do this and I can't do that.

JIT: I can't.

A sense of being worn out and tired

JIT: They take me to the hospital.

JIT: We can't make her better so someone will have to look after her. *(She hears them say.)* Only one daughter is there; she can't look after me.

JIT: I go to a place where lots of other people are the same as me. We just look at each other. They all have their mouths open and they are dripping. Maybe I am too. I can't feel it; my left side does not move.

Thinks back to her hospital visits with her daughter.

JIT: A thorn in my side. That daughter comes and visits.

Feeling rather sad with her voice

JIT: I am in bed. They keep me in bed. I cannot get out of bed. I look at her and see nothing in her eyes. I can't speak. I can't move.

Quiet voice and deep breaths as she thinks about her condition

JIT: Everything hurts but I can't tell them.

JIT: I see members of my family coming through the window. They pop in and have a look at me in the bed.

(Spirits.)

Pauses

JIT: My daughter pokes my left side.

Speaks fast now as though she is being hurried

JIT: Go on, off you go. *Hurry up* she says, *it is your time. Go on… go and see your family.* I close my eyes and wish myself to see my family.

She says with sadness

JIT: But I don't go.

Her voice represents resentment now

JIT: Every day she comes and pokes me in my left side.

Go   Go   Go

Pause

JIT: I have had enough now and I am tired of life.

She brightens up now as things are seen from a different perspective

JIT: I look at the daughter now from above. I look at her sitting at the bed.

JIT: She cries now; it is too late for crying.

The past is reflected in her voice

JIT: She was always my thorn in my side. She poked me and wanted me to go. I have gone now. Why was she crying?

Deep breaths

JIT: So, that is why I am looking at the hole in the ground because I was released from the body.

Happy and chirpy voice; it sounds so much younger

JIT: Now I am a happy little soul dancing around looking at everything that is going on.

JIT: Why are they crying?

JIT: What are they doing this for?

JIT: Why are they doing that?

JIT: I have loads of questions to ask.

JIT: Then I am pulled back into the dark.

JIT: They have finished now.

JIT: I am pulled back into the dark. I try and resist and pull forward. I can't. I can't go forward. I go back and up and away. Rising above, moving along.

Informative

JIT: That is how I arrived at the screen.

A pause and a thoughtful, reminiscing voice

JIT: There was always something wrong with the left side of my body; it never quite felt right.

JIT: Work it out for yourselves. (to the reader.)

JIT: I am going now.

Very strong in voice now

JIT: Some red orbs are coming to collect me.

JIT: I am red.

Ques: Are you red?

JIT: I am red.

Pause...

Said meaningfully but not loud

JIT: Jupiter.

JIT: Jupiter and Mars.

JIT: Where am I going?

JIT: Jupiter or Mars? Saturn or Uranus?

JIT: I might want to do some planet hopping.

A very long pause

JIT: Experiments...

JIT: Hologrammed into a laboratory.

JIT: I don't understand, but I do now.

JIT: They take me out of there and they take me into the library. The books are so big I hover by the side. Gain all the knowledge of any book at any particular time. (*Suggesting that the books transfer the knowledge as opposed to reading them.*)

Ques: What are the books?

JIT: Knowledge.

Ques: Do they have a name?

JIT: Knowledge books!

JIT: Knowledge books past, present and future.

JIT: I am taking knowledge from the future.

JIT: I am taking knowledge from the present.

JIT: I am taking knowledge from the past. It is all now.

JIT: I am bringing it all with me to the laboratory.

Pause

More upbeat statements

JIT: Experiments that happen on earth are being changed; people on earth do not understand how they are being changed.

JIT: It is called divine intervention.

JIT: We will change, we will move, we will eradicate, we will stop.

JIT: We will stop the people who create the problems.

JIT: There will be unknown causes of the deaths of the masses.

JIT: We **will** have intervened.

JIT: You are safe my children.

Ques: What, me and Jan?

JIT: Yes.

JIT: 12 years from the day.

Deep breaths

JIT: Divine intervention.

JIT: The forests will grow, the forests will grow, the trees are vast, everything is abundant; life is abundant.

Speaks at speed now

JIT: Everything grows two-fold, three-fold, four-fold, five-fold, six-fold…

JIT: The earth is nourished, we will nourish the earth, we will send down the nourishment for the earth.

JIT: We will nourish the earth.

Ques: Who is *we*?

Upbeat voice

JIT: We the reds.

JIT: Think of us injecting the centre of the earth and your little minds will understand. Think of us injecting the centre of the earth and watch as they inject. Divine intervention will give you this.

Voice changes, slows down to be meaningful and proud to be red

JIT: Why are things growing so fast? Why are things changing? We the reds will sort that.

JIT: We are 5.

Ques: Just 5?

In a raised voice

JIT: We are 5!

JIT: No one can stop it. No one can change it.

JIT: It is; it will be what it is. It is your destiny; it is the destiny.

JIT: It is the unknown, but we know. (*Proud that the reds know*)

JIT: There is a race that finishes; horses will die and bones will be broken, animals will crash to the ground.

Empathy in voice

JIT: Earthlings will feel so sad and not understand.

JIT: But I am telling you now, this will happen and the reason will be shown. Evolution is taking place.

Very fast methodical speech

JIT: Be guided by that star, the one that shines so bright, you look at that star and be guided. Drink from its brightness to give you energy and delight as you move forward in your life.

JIT: Your life on earth, I am talking about. Feed from the bright star.

Takes some deep breaths

JIT: That star and be guided by it.

JIT: They will launch it 2 more times. You watch as it blows up in the sky; they will launch it two more times. There will be an explosion as the rocket is launched.

JIT: Underground, the Russians think they have the key.

JIT: Look at the boundaries as they fade and fall; the key will be no longer there. We have the keys. Russia will fall.

Ques: Who is *we*?

Raised voice

JIT: We the reds!

The voice stops

JAN:

As I come out of trance I felt like I was slobbering! Maybe the left side of Margaretta?

Can you see how she referred to her daughter as a pain in her side? She then went on to have problems on her left side and on her death bed too, her daughter was poking her in her left side. So the pain in the side was there throughout her life.

Coincidence or not?

Do you think she could have changed this?

Is there a common thread through your life?

Once again as the soul passes, it takes its eternal life and loses all the earthly traits.

A little insight into the future is given towards the end of the dialogue.

■ ■ ■

Sessions 4-8

The following sessions 4-8 took on a slightly different tangent. We are looking into the spirit world and earth as an observer not from a passed soul's perspective.

Jan goes very deep in trance with stronger and more authoritative energies. Guiding us into the future with possible insights.

(Ques asks about Lightworkers, this is her earthly term. A lightworker has been defined by someone as "Anyone who devotes their life to being a bright light in the world. They understand their actions without ego may have the potential to raise the vibrations of earth.)

04 Trance

25-Jan-2016

Present in the room

JIT: Jan in trance

JAN: Jan as Jan

Ques: Asking the questions

Jan makes herself comfortable and begins to take herself into her altered trance state for this connection to channel their voice.

JAN: As I settle into trance, I have to tell you what I see; I asked to be surrounded by love and light as I begin my work. Straight away I received the most autonomous pink swirling around me which is my colour for love in my spiritual work. I am feeling very emotional...

Jan goes deeper into her altered state

JAN: I think it is going to be babies. I say that because I can see those see-through cots on wheels that they have in UK maternity hospitals.

JAN: I have a dreadful feeling in the pit of my stomach as I go deeper into trance... I have many rising emotions. I think this has held me back a little and they stepped in.

JAN: I was told not to be me and let go.

Slowly goes deep into that altered state

Takes some time to be where she needs to be

Speaks quietly

JIT: Malfunctioning, they all malfunctioned and I think it was all meant to be. Some malfunction.

A long pause here

Very softly and slowly spoken

JIT: It is time to come back; come on it is time for you all to come back now.

JIT: Like little sheep, follow me.

A distasteful sound is heard

JIT: Argghhh.

JIT: Come on. You cannot change anything. Come on. Come on with me.

Spoken in a whisper

JIT: Come on, come on... Come and find the other half... come on and find the whole soul.

JIT: Come on, fragmented at birth.

A slightly stronger voice

JIT: Malfunction.

JIT: Termination missed carriage... miscarriage. That's what you call it.

JIT: Experiments on foetuses that are underdeveloped.

JIT: They must stop now. The souls are troubled souls; a troubled soul remains the foetus that grows. Fragments of the troubled soul remain in the foetus in the laboratory, in the jar that is dissected that is experimented upon.

JIT: Troubled soul split.

JIT: The soul that remains and grows will always be known as the troubled soul until it is reunited with the fragments that are misplaced. Fragments can be misplaced before birth, after and some at the same time.

JIT: Those souls are not whole souls; they are troubled souls.

JIT: I collect those souls from the experiments from the laboratories all over the world, all over earth. I collect those souls.

Ques: And who are you?

JIT: Soul collector the regenerator.

Ques: Do you have a name?

JIT: You will know me in the angelic form.

Ques: What is the name of the angelic form?

Raises voice here and firmly states

JIT: Just know that I am the regenerator. I have no name that is earthly given.

Speaks slowly now and returns to a quiet voice

JIT: I look after the archangels and show them the way.

JIT: The archangels may collect the souls and bring them to me; they sit in the pods, traumatised and dysfunctional. I will revive.

JIT: They see the pods all around the room, each little fragment of a soul sitting happily in the pod.

JIT: On earth the troubled soul goes through life as a troubled soul. These are the ones who need to be saved; these are the ones who need the...

Very pronounced speech

JIT: E D U C A T I O N education.

JIT: These are the ones that need to break free from what you call family. These are also the ones, or so I have heard, that are called **black sheep** in families. They are the troubled souls; they will go on to do great things. They must break away from their earthly families to enable this.

JIT: On doing this, their fragmented soul will join them periodically, to show them the way, to give them guidance and to let their uniqueness shine. Brightly.

Until they break free they will be a troubled soul.

Breathes deep and recites the following in a demanding, raised voice

JIT: I am master of all divine of all the souls, the troubled souls, the fragmented souls. I create the space for the troubled souls to access when they break free. It is easy to access when they take their mind into the black and the dark, they take their **mind** into the atmospheric places and they look for their fragments.

JIT: They can feed off their fragments. They can talk to their fragments. They can ask for their fragments to join them when they need help. They will have broken ties with the family, the earthly family. The troubled soul will move forward and shine.

JIT: I will show you the flow like in a river, dancing and moving through their life with ease. Link back to the troubled soul and link back to the family and you will be **stuck** in that place. Not able to access your fragments.

JIT: Access the fragments and you will shine.

A bright, questioning tone

JIT: Deliver us from evil? There is no evil, just look for the balance, look for the balance because if you are off balance, it is not so good; if you are on balance, it is really good.

JIT: Look for your fragments to visit and come in the room that I survey.

JIT: Your mind will take you, just be still and allow it to happen. Your fragments are in the pods until you join them. Then, and only then, will you be fully united; that is the whole soul together.

JIT: Up until then it is visits. You, to the soul fragment, and the soul fragment to you.

Upbeat

JIT: Some people tell stories that these are the guardian angels coming to look after you.

Pffftt.

JIT: It is your fragmented soul.

Breathes deeper and connects to what seems to be a different... someone

Faster pace with an upbeat feeling

JIT: Journey to the centre of the earth. You can, you know, you can journey to the centre of the earth.

Ques: Are you still the guardian of the soul?

JIT: Who?

Ques: Who are you?

Ques: May I ask who you are?

Ignored the question

JIT: I am showing you the journey to the centre of the earth. I am showing you Pluto; there was an invasion. Plutonians invaded.

JIT: There is life on the planets, you know.

JIT: You need to look and only certain people will be shown. Only certain ones will see. They will be shown to the minds of the people.

JIT: They will be shown to the minds of the people who can see… see the visions through the orbs. Connect to a Doppelgänger and they will show you. But only a certain few will be taken to the planets.

JIT: Listen to the heartbeat and slow the heartbeat. Anyone can do this, and you can too; slow your mind and be taken.

JIT: Anyone can do this, only the chosen one will.

Spoken slowly

JIT: Slow your mind and be taken to the places where the heart beats.

JIT: Be alone, be sacrificial; be alone on your journey and see the triumphant future that is in front. Be alone.

JIT: Must now go and teach the young ones and show them the way; teach the young ones, they will be there for the future.

A long pause is taken

JIT: The palace with the underground tunnels and rooms will be filled with water.

JIT: The underground rooms of the palace will be no more. The smug person who owns the palace will be no more.

JIT: Deliver us from evil for thine is the kingdom the power and the glory. They will not have the power or the glory; they will cease. Generations from before will be freed, generations in the mountains will be freed.

JIT: Look out for the alignment; the alignment is near. Feel the shift and watch the planets align.

Loud voice repeats

JIT:

1 2 3 align

1 2 3 align

1 2 3 align

Becomes softer now

JIT: Three shifts straight after each other will happen. You look and you will see. No earthlings will know or feel what is happening, only those born.

Long pause

JIT: Be brave and show the world your findings; be brave my children.

Strong voice

JIT: Ten-fold, I say ten-fold.

JIT: Ten-fold will be the growth.

JIT: Ten-fold will be the abundance.

JIT: You wait, my children; ten-fold will be the abundance sold.

Jan begins to rock back and forth, her voice is strong and powerful now, almost rhythmic

JIT: Unity and diligence is the key, unity and diligence.

JIT: Uniqueness and foreboding energy **is** the key.

JIT: Christ was born, they say.

JIT: Was Christ born?

JIT: Is Christ there?

JIT: Who is Christ?

JIT: The questions will be asked; the questions are asked.

JIT: You go in your own unique way; you do not listen or read from what the others have decided.

JIT: I will show you.

JIT: Tenfold I say, tenfold.

Jan stops rocking back and forth

JIT: Look out for the Aries ram, I say no more.

JAN:

I closed my eyes and knew that I would not go into trance as easy as I normally do. I think I was disturbed, seeing the babies in the cots made me wonder what I was going to be shown. I was trying to bypass them with my earthly thoughts. Once I let go and trusted, I was able to trance.

A lesson here for those who have been labelled *black sheep* and a *troubled soul,* to let go of all who label you and the label itself. Learn how to connect to your other soul fragments and allow guidance. Clearly they are speaking of meditation and how it calms the mind and slows the heartbeat. This will then enable you to live your life as intended.

I felt they did not want to be Ques-tioned today as they did not answer or get in to a conversation with Ques.

■ ■ ■

05 Trance

27-Jan-2016

Present in the room

JIT: Jan in trance

JAN: Jan as Jan

Ques: Asking the questions

Jan makes herself comfortable and begins to take herself into her altered trance state for this connection to channel their voice.

JAN: As I walk into the room today, something feels different although it is exactly as it has always been. Maybe there are different energies around. As I am going down into trance, I feel like I want to hold onto the blanket that I put around me; I feel anxious, scared and a little frightened

That is where I am starting... I am going deeper now.

Spoken in a meaningful and informative way

JIT: You all keep looking for the light. Every time you look for the light; the light is not important. It is all around you. Don't focus on the one thing that is not going to give you what you are looking for.

JIT: Sometimes we give the light, sometimes we don't. It does not matter.

Mockingly said

JIT: Did they see the light? Where is the light?

JIT: When you see the brightness of white, it is not a light, it is brightness. It is a beautiful place, a space that we can take you to, but it is brightness, not a light.

JIT: It is brightness, not the light; you are not being guided to the light, up to the light, or in the light.

JIT: We are creating a space of brightness.

Long pause here and brightly says

JIT: Killer queen and the magical mystery tours, they had it right.

A long pause

JIT: Release your selves from the restraints that you have put around; only you have done that and your fore fathers and mothers. Cut the restraints, cut the shackles and release yourselves.

JIT: Cut the restraints; now is the time, now.

JIT: Move on to the place that you need to be. Move forward, move forward but stay where you are. Move forward but stay where you are; that is right.

JIT: You are staying in that position but different things are happening around you.

JIT: If you work hard, you can see the energy fields on everything. Know that everything has an energy field. *(Moving closer to some rocks.)* If you look hard enough you will see them quiver. You can almost walk inside the rock because they will change to the eyes of the chosen few; they will change.

JIT: You can see spheres beyond; atmospherics will play a different part if you see through the rocks because they will take on a different form.

JIT: Schools know that things need to change now; they have been told. You won't know that, but they have.

JIT: They need to change, they need to up their act, they need to embrace the future of what has been seen and shown to them.

JIT: Some schools will fail and fall, some will excel.

I feel a different energy is taking over and talking with fast speech

JIT: Dynamite is here to stay. Don't get crushed in the stampede of the people thinking they know where they are going, thinking they know what they want.

Breathes to becomes a calmer energy

JIT: You will rise above; you will rise above and see the beauty all around. You will be in that beautiful place. To continue the rest of your journey, do not get caught in the stampede. Hold back, stand by the side, rise above; do not get with the stampede.

JIT: There will be so many failures and you will hear people using the words, *failing this* and *failing that*.

Exhales deeply and says:

JIT: It is all earthly.

JIT: Geomantus is the one, Geomantus I see, Geomantus I say, go I will rise.

JIT: Geomantus will rise from the sands when they crack. Geomantus will rise and give you, the chosen ones, the direction in which to move.

JIT: You can salute me now because you know I will be right, so salute me now.

Ques: Who are you to salute?

There is no answer and a long pause

A different energy speaks now, meaningfully quiet and a little muffled

There are quiet voices but nothing to decipher. Soft and gentle

JIT: Where there is no water there will be.

JIT: Where there is no rain there will be.

JIT: From below, the water will come and nourish the people, the flowers and the food. From below, the water will come.

JIT: Gallons of water below will fill and rise. Fill and rise with a heartbeat in the body will fill and rise.

Very muffled and sounds like an old person

JIT: Never fear we don't have enough, never fear.

Long pause

The same voice continues

JIT: Don't understand. When I look at the hospitals and I see people sitting in rooms attached to medicine, medicine being poured through their veins making them ill, they are ill. Two ills do not make well.

JIT: Why does this happen?

The voice feels so sad

JIT: Why do people on earth think they can kill the already dying?

JIT: Why is this right?

This paragraph is spoken very slowly

JIT: There are ways that you should look at to prevent such illnesses in the body from happening. Begin to look at prevention. Prevention is the cure. Do not feed the condition.

Pause

Jan turns in her chair and faces the other way

A long pause

JIT: The governments will begin to crumble.

JIT: People will die in the governments; they will be replaced by the chosen ones.

A long pause and deep breathing

JIT: I can hear the war, the war, the war of the worlds. Not too many wars, just the people will be eradicated sooner than you think. Looking forward into the future there will be no random shootings or bombs.

JIT: Remember we have spoken of this before, just wait and you will be shown, just wait my friends.

JIT: Try not to analyse my little ones, just wait and all will be there; we will tell you, we will give you the answers now and in the future.

JIT: You just work in the way we are giving it to you, not what you think you should be doing.

A pause

JIT: The eyes will see. Who will make new eyes for people? Who will be changed? Eyes will see. Eyes will see the difference; eyes will see the way forward and the changes.

JIT: Calm your minds to find the answers, dear friends.

JAN:

I quickly came back into the room and remember feeling out of sorts. I realised was facing the opposite way on my chair. There seemed to be a lot of deep information coming in quickly into my mind.

More suggestions of Meditation and letting go of conditioning; the message to let go of conditioning is very strong. To not spend time looking for the light and accept all that is. They touched on energy vibrations here too.

Also there was not much response to Ques-tioning.

■ ■ ■

06 Trance

27-Jan-2016

Present in the room

JIT: Jan in trance

JAN: Jan as Jan

Ques: Asking the questions

Jan makes herself comfortable and begins to take herself into her altered trance state for this connection to channel their voice.

JAN: I can see a volcano; I am inside and there are pockets of safety with the lava bubbles. Looking up I can see via the vortex of eruption to the sky above.

Working her way further into her altered state of trance

JIT: There will be communication without speaking, there will be telepathic communication. People will be learning the telepathy.

JIT: Ancient Greeks, they had the keys. The ancient Greeks and the different lands had the keys to open the doors. They had the key to allow more to be seen; so many things are locked away on earth.

JIT: On earth as it is in heaven.

JIT: The keys will be retrieved; you don't need the keys now.

A light and informative voice

JIT: Architecture will change, sacred sites will reveal more, and they will alter the course of history in a dramatic way.

JIT: So far you have seen dribs and drabs of this happening; now the dramatic changes will be seen and the contradictions to the books that have been written generations and generations before.

JIT: We will show; we will give the information as the sacred sites reveal more; they will reveal things that will make the current laughable.

JIT: Learn the telepathic way of communication. Be mindful of everything around you, be mindful of the space, your space; be mindful of all. Go to the sacred sites, my friends, and touch the earth beneath. Take your mind into the earth and see the changes, see the changes in your mind's eye. You can do it. You can do it.

JIT: She has before.

Ques: Who is she?

JIT: The one I talk with.

They refer to Jan

JIT: Seven

Spoken at speed

JIT: See them stand up straight, see them upright by the gate.

JIT: We don't go back; we open up more. We open up more paths, we open up more communication. Will open up the vision... will open up what was once created for that time.

JIT: Now that time has come again. We will need the advanced corrections on the things that were created.

The following dates are given

JIT: 1549, 1312, 1210, AD10.

JIT: Look at what happened around those times, they will be repeated with advanced communications and technological interference.

JIT: Open the tombs and look within.

JIT: You will see. You will see.

Large intakes of breath to continue in this informative way

JIT: Open the tombs, my friends, and see what is inside; now is the time to reveal all. Say a prayer if it makes you feel better, but no need. Open the tombs and share.

JIT: Jerusalem will feature wide.

JERUSALEM!

JIT: *The Americas are joined as one...* (Jan gesticulates as if to join the boundaries.)

JIT: The Americans have no boundaries; this will be renamed.

JIT: As will Brazil and Russia, they will be renamed. They will be no more as they are today. Africa falls into the sea.

JIT: Asia is the key, look at **Asia** rising.

JIT: Hieroglyphics will be changed.

JIT: Look at the hieroglyphics, see the lions and the tigers; we will change those pictures to a different symbol and everything will make sense.

JIT: Someone will realise the hieroglyphics need to be altered, turned around turned upside down, or inside out, and they will then make perfect sense. They will show you the way of now.

Ques: Who are you?

Said softly

JIT: I am here to speak today.

Continues in a slow speech

This is a different energy

JIT: We sit in the room and we look at the planets.

JIT: We realign, we begin to realign and I have it all in my control. I am the one that is being guided to realign the planets to make the saviour of the earth.

JIT: Without the realignment, without the shift, without the new wave of children and people on earth, earth will fold and crumble and be blasted…

Speaks loud and very strong

JIT: From the centre in to smithereens, all going out into space. Follow the directions and you will survive. You are destined to survive.

JIT: Those causing havoc and pandemonium will not survive. They will live on earth, but not as they know it now. They will be sectioned to the other side, the dark side of the earth.

JIT: No daytime light shall shine on that place.

Long pause now

Very deep in and exhales

This is a different energy, very strong and direct

JIT: Watch over the archangels and the arch masters. I watch them and instruct them; they work as I ask them to, they know what is to be done. They know their job.

Pause

JIT: Drink the nectar with the thumb, the nectar of yesteryears. Drink the nectar with the thumb.

JIT: Clear the roots and chakras.

JIT: Allow all vortexes to spin with balance, allow the balance to come from within. Keep on now and make that earthly body capable of all that it is designed to do.

Speaking very fast, strongly pronouncing each word

JIT: Make that earthly body capable for the future, make it resonate, make the spiral spin so that everyone can be moved out of your way to enable you to **attack**... *Breathe*

Spoken slowly

JIT: ...the future.

Long pause

JIT: Receive the healing given at night, receive.

Deep exhale, creating more connections

A change of energy, this is a lighter one but with a firm voice

JIT: As you lay in your beds the chosen ones receive the reprogramming as it comes from the room, from the space beyond. I watch as you sleep; I watch as you recharge.

JIT: Group gatherings are perfect. Group gatherings with meditation will allow me to enhance anything that is done within the groups. Allow me to enter and make the changes in the brain waves.

JIT: To make the changes in the thought patterns.

JIT: To make the changes in the correspondence.

JIT: To make the changes for the future of the people.

JIT: Most people will survive; they are the chosen ones.

Deeply inhales

JIT: Earth is green, earth is brown. Earth is blue and earth is yellow.

JIT: Merge it all together and live in the beautiful space that we will create.

Is it flat or is it round?

Small pause

Faster pace

JIT: Pluto is like a bouncing ball… will jump to earth and back again. Watch as the planets collide in the future.

JIT: It is just an exchange of energy. Those with the scopes will think it amazing. It is just an exchange of energy. No harm will come.

JIT: Balls of fire will be seen in space. That's all, balls of fire. Calm your minds, dear ones, and allow the healers to heal.

Pausing and exhaling

JAN: As I am coming back, I want to sing that song... *Go Johnny go! Go Johnny be good*.

Although Jan seems to be coming back and speaks to the Ques, she adds the following.

Spoken very quickly and drops back into altered state

JIT: I can see the beach, black and white dog, someone with a house on the beach.

JIT has the vision of this person

JIT: Glass house on the beach, person playing the piano, looking out to sea. The windows of the house are all panoramic, to see the beautiful landscape.

JIT: The glass windows open. Looking through the open window they are looking at the sky.

JIT: There is something coming out of the sky? Or they are taking them into the sky?

JIT: Someone from that house will disappear.

JIT: It is a man. I feel a well-known person. He is not very tall, pointed nose, straight short hair. Black trousers. Long sleeved white t-shirt.

JIT: Playing the piano... doors open and he goes out, something happens...

JAN:

The main thread for this dialogue is the chakra, vortex and healing along with the thoughts of changing things that have existed for many years.

Meditation and telepathy are featured again.

Or are we being shown that we need to change the way we see things?

The dialogue stopped abruptly.

Very little with Ques.

■ ■ ■

07 Trance

29-Jan-2016

Present in the room

JIT: Jan in trance

JAN: Jan as Jan

Ques: Asking the questions

Jan makes herself comfortable and begins to take herself into her altered trance state for this connection to channel their voice.

JIT: Telecommunications and telepathy, help the young ones to develop this.

JIT: I can see some screens. Looking at the small screens, I am taken through a vortex.

Searching for what is being shown

JIT: On the screens, I know are the chakras of the people on earth; it has to be.

JIT: I see the vortex within their bodies. They are spinning in different directions; not everyone is spinning the same. People are lining up for something and I can see through the skin. I can see into the bodies. I can see the energy; it is building up in the body.

JIT: Something… some of the vortexes have alien matter inside them; it is like they have been programmed. It is my job to take it out. From here behind the screen, I am able to take the intrusions in the body.

JIT: Intrusions out of the body.

Ques: Implants?

JIT: No

JIT: They are not implants, they are obstructions.

JIT: They are not **creating**; they are stopping creation.

JIT: On the screens, I am taking out the objects that are stopping the vortexes from spinning correctly. I do not have to be with the people. I can take them out remotely.

JIT: As I take 1 out, 2 out, 3 out of different people who are queuing up for something; I don't know what they are queuing up for.

JIT: I am taking out the implants… (*Ques had asked if they were implants, and* **JIT** *said no, but now they call them implants… I feel they are but only by the* *nature that they are implanted, not as Ques reference to them implied.)*

JIT: I move forward in the queue.

JIT: What are they queuing up for?

Tuts as she can't see why they are queuing.

JIT: People are moving forward but I can't see what they are moving forward to.

JIT: They keep switching between me watching on the screen, me being the person doing the work and me in the queue.

JIT: I have become the orb that I have been previously, the observing orb; like the visitor, I am allowed to be there.

JIT: I have been here before; I have seen it before.

JIT: I am asking what it is they are doing in the queue. I am not shown; all I get is like x-ray vision to the spirals/vortex.

JIT: I can see as the foreign bodies are taken out, the people move forward. I can't see where they go.

The voice speeds up now

JIT: I am the visiting orb.

Talking from the orb's perspective

JIT: I can see 4 screens.

JIT: He is in charge of all the screens.

JIT: There are different queues on all the screens.

JIT: He is working on the chakra/vortex; he is working on them. Then they move forward and I can't see where they go; it is like they have gone through the queue.

JIT: Somewhere…

JIT: I feel once his work is done, they go back into their lives. He takes me out and encourages me to follow him.

JIT: There is no voice, I just know.

JIT: He takes me out.

JIT: We are bobbing along in the universe. It feels like I am moving, but I don't think I am.

JIT: Another screen room begins to emerge in the black, a hologram room…

JIT: I am in a school. School children are eating a meal; I can see a tray with bits of food on, and pills are given to the children. This is to come in schools, not all schools though, as it is control.

JIT: This person who speaks with me will take away that control.

JIT: Different schools are shown on the screens.

Raised voice

JIT: Look into the minds of the children. Erasing something from the minds of the children.

Normal voice returns

JIT: It looks like he is performing brain work, an intricate operation; he is working on the brains through the screens. We are moving out of the schools.

JIT: On the screens the visual is an aeroplane. There is something in the food that the people are eating. Not everyone has it; the people that sit in certain seats have a "force field" around them and they are exempt from the food. They try, but they can't physically give it to them.

JIT: There are two types of people, those who can and those who can't.

JIT: I am exiting the plane.

JIT: Another room is emerging; I am waiting for it to develop. I am with the same orb. There is no verbal communication, but I know I have to stay and wait as I know we will go into the room.

Waits patiently

JIT: I am being shown what looks like a doctor's surgery and I see this on the screen.

Long pause

Quickly spoken

JIT: I am in the surgery; it is robotic.

JIT: It is different to an earthly surgery.

JIT: I am looking into the surgery through the screens.

JIT: Robotic, no human receptionist. Very robotic.

JIT: I am sensing that bodies are scanned as they come into the surgery.

JIT: The screen shows one scanner, then a different one; I feel there are different depths of scanning.

JIT: I can see; they are looking for something within the bodies. The people move through the scanner and some go off to the left and some go off to the right.

JIT: A couple of people move forward and I see they have another scanner to go through. The majority are going in the forward direction after the scanner.

JIT: It's gone... (reference to the room.)

Pause, and deeper breathing

Sentences said with pauses in-between

JIT: I feel I am in churches but I want to say places of religious worship.

JIT: Not churches as I know them; the leader is being replaced and the leader is not the leader.

JIT: The person giving the service or giving instruction is not the person being replaced.

JIT: A bit like a robot with skin.

Can hear the words...

JIT: Control the masses.

JIT: As people come out of these buildings.

A little mixed up and feeling the confusion in the voice

There are people in the church like buildings

JIT: Whilst they are inside the buildings, the walls change.

JIT: I can see psychedelic colours being spun in different directions and projected on to the walls. Colours and shapes transfiguring to create a kaleidoscope effect. The people look at them, their eyes closed, and they can see the colours.

JIT: This all has a prescribed effect on the people.

JIT: As I come out of the building, there are three choices to the left, right and forward directions.

The voice is stronger and has urgency

JIT: Looking on the screens, I see the church like buildings. One has only 3 people exiting and they all go to the left. Another building has 150 people and most go to the right. There are other buildings and those people exit in various directions.

Loud voice says the one word

JIT: Sorting.

Not much emotion attached to it

JIT: As the building becomes empty, the filters on the lights are changed. The psychedelic sequence is different for the next set of people.

JIT: The sequence of the filter light patterns is something to do with... *(I am not shown what.)* Those people who go out never come back in again and they never... *(I am not shown.)*

JIT: Each congregation has a different filter pattern.

JIT: All the time I can see this on the screens and I am not in the physical location.

JIT: I do feel control.

As Jan tries to describe the people changing the filter, the planets pop into vision.

JIT: Pluto and Jupiter.

JIT: It has gone now, the room with the church like screens.

Long pause now

JIT: With the same person, I am not moving, and not travelling at all. I am static and the rooms are coming to me. The holograms come closer as they develop.

In a loud voice

JIT: Transportation ground!

And back to describing the scene

JIT: I am looking through the screens. I can see different types of cars and trains; not like we know them; it is amazing. They are so different.

JIT: The music, the music in the cars and buses and trains.

JIT: The people on the ground are on a calling, they are all going to the same place, and as they travel, the music plays in their vehicle. They are asked to listen to the music.

JIT: The music is playing now.

Spoken in a robotic way

JIT: Subliminal congestion, subliminal overload, subliminal traction.

JIT: One person stops their car and steps out and won't listen to the music and so does someone else and a few more. They put their fingers in their ears in a bid to stop the sound penetrating to their brain. They talk to each other to drown out the sound but their words cannot be heard.

JIT: Everyone else continues to the same place.

JIT: I am looking at this through the screens. I feel like the orb is smiling at me; it is a knowing feeling. He knows what he is doing. All these people keep going forward in their different transportation modes. They are going to the sea; we can see the sea in the screens.

JIT: I am in the Orbie room looking on the screens; I am looking from the sea towards the land. A mass of sea, then land, and I can see the people coming from all directions to the seashore.

JIT: I know there is some kind of...

JIT: Because I am in the sea or sending something into the sea.

JIT: There is some kind of magnetic probe going into the sea that sends out all these... it is like...

JIT: I want to say dancing...

Urmmm, breathes out with frustration

As Jan can't seem to describe it as it is out of earthly bounds as we know it

JIT: The water begins to dance on a different vibration; this vibration goes through, albeit under the water. The surface does not change its appearance.

JIT: Under the water there is a dancing vibration.

Very fast speech

JIT: When I look under the water, but from the screen, I can see people's legs and feet going into the water.

JIT: I can't see on top of the sea now.

JIT: Magnetic vibration and pulses underneath the water are drawing the people in.

JIT: I can see their feet, knees and thighs. They are walking into the water.

Takes a breath...

Pauses a little

Statement

JIT: I don't know where they go.

JIT: It just stops. He looks at me again. I have this sense of, you know... like I know where they are going.

JIT: I am thanking him because I feel honoured to be with him.

JIT: I feel very tearful.

Jan sounds emotional

JIT: And it feels so special.

Very emotional, tranquil

JIT: Whatever they are doing, going into the water is so special for them.

JIT: *I want to say they are going home...* (Jan is tearful in the trance.)

JIT: A bit like a mass exodus, but so calm. So beautiful.

JIT: So amazingly beautiful.

JIT: Thank you.

Jan composes herself

Pause

JIT: That scene finishes.

JIT: I feel movement.

JIT: I can see flashes of lights in the distance. I feel movement as I look down to the side; I can see shards of brightness, but I don't know what it is.

Fast speech

JIT: It is like I am being taken to some sort of platform, hovering and looking in forward. I feel what I have been on was lower; I am now higher perspective.

JIT: Looking into... I feel the words...

JIT: Whole New World.

JIT: A Subsection of earth is being created.

JIT: A Subsection of the universe is being created.

JIT: A Subsection of eternal beings are being manifested as we speak.

Very determined voice

JIT: Zero, the clock started ticking at **zero**; the clock ticks at zero, still on zero.

JIT: It is not ready to be set in place yet... it is going to happen.

JIT: Jupiter, Pluto.

JIT: So I just sit here and look; he shows me to look. Most things are black. I can see the shape of what I feel is earth a long way in the distance. I can see and hear Pluto, Saturn and Jupiter; the words, not the planets.

JIT: He is putting thoughts in my head; he says don't think, just talk.

JIT: I am doing!

JIT: 2026... year 2026 will be a switching on, connecting to, and aligning with the planets of succession.

JIT: The planets will grow and transport between them will develop.

JIT: For the chosen ones, I emphasise again that telecommunication is key to get your house in order; your house is you.

JIT: Your soul requirements will be revealed to you.

JIT: My dear young ones listen to your soul; your soul is important more so now than ever before. Everyone has theirs; it **does** talk to you, it **does** show you the way, it **does** give you clues. Its existence in the body needs to be fulfilled; keep moving my dear ones, keep moving forward. Open the doors and feel. What do you feel? Go by you and no one else. Be led by yourself; you are unique and will shine bright.

A deep and strong voice...

JIT: Endeavour to take the paths that are the dark ones; you will stay there; you will not return. Your soul knows this, so listen to your soul.

JAN:

This was a very emotional trance. I felt a little uneasy and when I returned had a feeling that I knew something but was not really aware of what it was.

There is so much more confirmation that we need to be looking after ourselves and the importance of listening to our soul's real purpose.

How do you feel after reading this dialogue?

I do notice that Ques did not ask any questions or speak to the voice.

■ ■ ■

08 Trance

29-Jan-2016

Present in the room

JIT: Jan in trance

JAN: Jan as Jan

Ques: Asking the questions

Jan makes herself comfortable and begins to take herself into her altered trance state for this connection to channel their voice.

JIT: Tokyo…

Deep breaths

Suddenly jumps in with a loud voice

JIT: Tokyo is here to stay; Tokyo will be swept away.

Exhales to move deeper into trance state

JIT: Looking through the fog.

JIT: Tokyo will be nervous.

JIT: Tokyo will try and control. Tokyo will hide. Tokyo buildings will come crashing down.

JIT: People will survive underground.

JIT: The whole of the county will be swept clear, cleaned, and the surface will be demolished.

JIT: Underground, world leaders will congregate there.

JIT: Rabbits in warrens will be smoked out. The rabbits in the warrens will not survive.

JIT: Tokyo land did not conform. The Tokyo land tried to escape, the Tokyo land is no more.

Said abruptly

JIT: Flattened.

Voice is slower and lower now; a different energy voice rises

JIT: The earth's vibrations will change; that area will be reconstructed and used for something that only the people from different lands will understand. Because they will visit, they will be taken there after the land is cleared.

Exhales deeper

JIT: Asia will continue to change. Asia's structures will be cleaned.

JIT: Asia's ancient structures will be redeveloped; the lands that were will become the lands that will be. The lands that will be for the future.

JIT: We will visit the sacred sites, my children.

The voice is raised and pronounced

JIT: There are no temples of **doom**.

JIT: There is no **doom;** earth's people's perception is **doom**. There is no **doom**.

JIT: You will live as you have been told to live. You will live as you have **chosen** to live; that will be your future, my dear friends.

A pause

JIT: The building that is hidden in the trees.

JIT: I see the vast forest with lush green trees, with a tall, red brick chimney protruding through the tree tops is the turret. A camera on the turret surveys the land, and people will see; it will be no more.

Pause and meaningful voice

JIT: The tides will change; the waters will fall.

JIT: The ice will stop. The land will become warm.

Pauses, said matter of fact

JIT: Seasons are no more.

Pause

JIT: All the important creatures and insects will stay; they will continue; they will be there for earth.

A pause... continues in an informative way

JIT: Descale your pineal gland, descale it.

JIT: Let it run free within your mind, let it run free. Free thinking is the key. Freedom and free world, free-will.

JIT: This can all be yours but not as you think it, not as you know it.

JIT: We will show you the way.

JIT: Everything now is just a process; not the same process as the one I show you from here.

JIT: We will open the doors, everything now will cease. It will change, it will not continue beyond this point; it will be changed.

JIT: Listen to us, don't use your minds and think; think only of what I tell you. Think only of the next time I need to communicate with you. Think only of these times.

Stronger voice speaks

JIT: Allow the goodness and the greatness to be developed with the interference.

Pause and posture change with deep exhale

JIT: Eradication will be happening.

Pause

Said boldly

JIT: Questions.

Ques: Who are you?

JIT: Does not matter. I have no earthly name.

Ques: What questions do I need to ask?

In a very quiet voice

JIT: You ask, I wait.

Ques: What preparations do we need to make?

JIT: Educate the children and show them the way, and fill your soul with goodness.

Ques: How do we do that?

Voice is raised now

JIT: Think only of the good.

JIT: Think only of the life you have; where you are, is where you are.

JIT: Where you want to be is where you are not.

JIT: Feed the soul from where you are.

JIT: Look for the goodness around you and feed your soul.

Ques: Is there anything else we need to do?

Ques jumps in with another question before they have time to answer

Ques: How do we educate the children?

JIT: You will be shown what to do.

JIT: You will be shown how to educate the children.

JIT: You will be given the tools to enable you to do this.

Ques: Is there any other work that needs to be done by us?

JIT: Listen and you will be shown, and act accordingly.

Ques: Are they any other preparations that need to be done?

Authoritative voice

JIT: All preparations will be shown to you in dreams and visions; please act up on these instructions.

JIT: Times 10.

Deep exhales waiting for the next question

JIT: Finished?

Ques: I think so; I can't think of anything else to ask.

JIT: Light-workers will unite.

Ques: Are we all light-workers?

Questioning voice and raised

JIT: All?

Ques: Everybody?

Ques: On earth?

JIT: No.

Ques: Am I a light-worker?

Ques: Is Jan a light-worker?

JIT: You are a light-worker. Jan is not.

JIT: You need to be open and receptive to the things I will show you.

JIT: You have plenty of learning; you have plenty of greatness to come in the future.

JIT: You are not ready yet, my child; you listen and you will be shown.

Ques: Will I find these things easy to do?

JIT: You will embrace everything that is given to you.

Ques: How will I be given these instructions, through dreams?

Ques: Or am I already bringing these things in?

JIT: You will be shown, you will understand; dreams, visions and synchronicities will show you the way. You will hear the person with a different voice. Listen and they will hold the key for the future.

JIT: Eradicate the knowledge so far and allow the new to come in.

JIT: Serpents at the gates will show you the way also. Serpents at the gates.

JIT: Transgender…

Ques: Who, me or someone else?

JIT: I will show you, the transgender, I will show you. The person is your teacher in the future.

Ques: Am I in the right place at the right time now?

JIT: Yes, my dear.

Voice softens

JIT: All is well

Ques: Will you speak to me again through Jan?

JIT: Yes, my child.

Ques: Thank you.

Ques: And all this work will be done to the highest and the best?

(They only work to the highest and best.)

Voice fades as though not wanting to answer

JIT: Yes, dear.

Ques: Is it time for you to go now?

Very low voice...

JIT: One more minute.

Ques: Is there more we need to know?

Very low voice, concentrating

JIT: I just have to look; wait, let me look at you.

JIT: Open up the channels of communication.

JIT: You must listen through your eyes.

Exhales deeply

Ques: Are you still looking at me?

Does not want to be interrupted, breathing indicates deep concentration

JIT: Yes.

JAN:

The voice did not say anymore. However, I had a wonderful sense of heat on one side of my body.

Healing was given to Ques. As I was taken inside the body, changes were made to the insides; taking out old and making way for new. Also creating tools for letting go and manifesting. There was a changing to the colours of the chakras as they were not correct. Beautiful silver strands were used for the connections that needed to be kept.

It was evident in this session that Ques seemed to be concerned about self, asking personal questions. The voice gave answers, but will Ques act upon them? Often we are shown the way in life but we choose not to make the changes.

I have actually performed this healing work in private healing sessions with excellent results.

■ ■ ■

Sessions 9-11

There is anticipation at the beginning of these sessions as Jan has been told by her guides to lie down for the following sessions. The room was changed and she lay on a therapy couch in her healing room, covered with a blanket. Instead of sitting in her usual chair. The room was prepared with candles, crystals and music before session 9 began.

Straight in are the voices with information for the future with hints of how we can help ourselves. Delivering further insights into our own perceptions of self.

09 Trance

01-Feb-2016

Present in the room

JIT: Jan in trance

JAN: Jan as Jan

Ques: Asking the questions

Jan makes herself comfortable and begins to take herself into altered trance state for this connection to channel their voice.

Straight in with the words in a stern voice

JIT: 2027 will see incredible power, power from the masses; it will be collective power.

A reassuring voice

JIT: Telepathy power.

JIT: Threats of Bombs like you have never seen before will not happen.

JIT: Back to earth and back to Mother Nature.

Pause

JIT: New channellings will be given to you.

Pause

Statements followed

JIT: North, south, east and west.

JIT: Take the beauty and mix it with all the rest.

JIT: Creations and co-recreations.

JIT: Diversity and deliverance.

Pauses, and voice is louder

JIT: What are the twisted worlds, twisted nations? The twisted and then entwined will untangle and grow.

JIT: Stop feeding the ailments and let them subside; stop feeding, giving energy and breathing to those that die. Don't give energy and breath to those that kill you.

Becomes breathless as reciting, and agitated

JIT: Some people's grief is insurmountable. Grief is but a transition; allow the transition to take place and all will be well.

JIT: Muffled is the voice that speaks to the people.

JIT: Ahhh.

JIT: Diocese will crumble.

JIT: They look as I show you down to the earth; they will all fall, the floors will open and reveal the chambers that were closed many years before.

A short pause

JIT: Pick up the rocks now and hold on to the energy. Keep the rocks because our life will depend upon the future vibrations that are given out daily. Hold on to the rocks and the future vibrations, my dear ones.

QUES: Whose dear ones, who are you?

Said in a rhythmic pattern

JIT: One and one is two

JIT: Two and two is four

JIT: Four and four is eight

JIT: Eight and eight is sixteen

JIT: Look out for the duplications, the synchronicity, the answers to the sums as they come to you, through unexpected sources.

JIT: Pick up the teaspoon; along the handle rub your finger.

Softly spoken

JIT: Creatures of the night will show their faces in the daylight. Creatures of the night will have new survival **instincts** for the future.

Long pause

Short statements in deep, connected voice

JIT: Tennessee sees all the children out of the schools running, shouting and screaming.

JIT: The beaches will be a pathway; people enter from the sea.

JIT: Lighthouses fall. There is no direction. People exit from the sea onto land, but people who walk **into** the sea from the land will experience the greatest of them all.

Direct knowing voice

JIT: Jingle bells the Christmas season, parting company with that one as well…

Long pause

JIT: I see the shootings out of the window of a silver Cadillac.

JIT: Earth will be reborn.

Long pause spoken as though feeling the torture

JIT: Torture

Pause

Spoken slowly

JIT: Torture and implements of war are hidden below the sands. Each president needs to look beneath to see, to see the answers to the questions. The presidents need to look and not be shocked by what they find.

Long pause faster speech

JIT: Take the key, my children, it will open up the world, for as you want it to be, it can be.

She speaks fast

JAN: I begin to come out of trance but I can't open my eyes. I want to know what I was talking about...

Ques: Explains a little.

JAN: I still can't open my eyes. I have to go deeper without coming fully out of the previous one.

Long pause

Begins to talk very slowly

JIT: Rip off, rip off, rip off.

JIT: Female statutes, the alabaster people will have their hands severed.

JIT: The sacred sites still hold the keys.

Very slowly spoken, with pauses

JIT: As the floors open up the sacred sites are changing; the floors will open up. Underneath the parts where nobody wants to change anything or move anything, the tiles they will lift to show you the way forward for the future.

JIT: All over the world there are sites almost changing together.

Speaks faster and louder

JIT: To deliver the information to the people, look at this information and be proud; you are part of this information. Information overload may take place, information overload.

JIT: Warning! Warning! Information overload!

JIT: No one can process what is seen; the visions are too much for people's brains.

JIT: Information overload!

Long pause spoken with speed

JIT: As the hearts beat faster interception, interception, interception, intervention. Long arms from the holograms will take over. The long arms of metal will be introduced, to the bellies of the people who need to release; they will be operated on with the long arms.

Slows down a little

JIT: Operations from the holograms are happening now to the people on earth and the other planetarium beings. Predominately earth. Earth's structure, earth's diversity, wars and those who try and control earth are all signs worked upon from the holograms.

Spoken very slowly and seems to be feeling this as she speaks it

JIT: Peel back the layers of time, move into the centre and feel and see and hear the nuggets of information that have passed people by because they were too busy to listen and see. Remember, you can hear with your eyes.

Ques: How can you hear with your eyes?

JIT: See all.

JIT: Feel and think all.

Said abruptly

JIT: Next.

JIT: Question.

Ques: How do you open up to the telepathy, how do you evolve the telepathy?

JIT: Practise, listen within and listen to your mind; listen to your instructions when you are ready. Instructions will be given.

JIT: Next question.

Ques: What keys are you talking about?

JIT: Keys... They are not the keys.

JIT: They are the openings and entrances to the new areas that will be revisited. I try and make the earthly words for understanding on the planet. Keys are used to unlock potential ways forward, that is why I use the word keys; not literal keys.

JIT: You will know.

Pauses

States

JIT: Question.

Ques: There is too much I have to try and digest. Will it all fall into place?

JIT: Not everyone will experience everything; everyone will have a place, everyone will have a learning, everyone will have movement, but not everyone will have everything.

JIT: Trust.

JIT: Question.

Ques: What is Jan's role in this and what is my role in this?

JIT: You are the lightworker as discussed before. My fellow worker will talk to you later.

Ques: And Jan?

JIT: She knows her work.

Ques: Does it have a name like lightworker?

JIT: No!

JIT: Question.

Ques: Jan and I working together, is this the right path that we are on?

Said in shock, you should know and trust this

JIT: Yes, of course, I brought you together to do this work, to enable the work to be done.

Ques: So each complements each other, the lightworker and Jan?

JIT: In earth terms, perhaps.

Ques: Is this working in unison, like this, happening all over the world, all over earth like me and Jan? So we can complete the bigger picture?

Pauses

JIT: Sometimes people, humans as the one you call Jan, are unable to execute everything alone.

Spoken in a robotic way

JIT: Another form of Jan will be creating very similar. They are very much a **lone** worker; they will always be a **lone** worker. They encounter people, predominantly lightworkers, who will give help and assistance to the work that they need to do at the guided time. They are also joined together with others who will enable them to move forward on their path.

Ques: Are lightworkers a lone worker or collective?

JIT: Collective, my dear one.

Ques: And humans like Jan are the loners?

JIT: Yes!

Spoken very slowly

JIT: You will **never** understand the things she sees and what she does. The information and visuals we will bring to her must be steady and slow so as not to take her into the place where she would sit and rock. We work closely and carefully with the human forms like the one you call Jan.

Ques: And who are you, who are the people who come to Jan? Is there an earthly name?

JIT: No, think of us as a voice.

Ques: Of more than one?

JIT: More than one what?

Raises voice as no answer comes

JIT: More than one what?

Ques raises voice

Ques: Energy, entity, being, a collective voice?

That question is ignored

Continues after a long pause

JIT: Question.

Ques: When you say people walk in to the sea, is that what was Atlantis, as we know it?

JIT: People walk in to the sea to find peace and harmony with their souls.

Ques: And what about the people coming from the sea to the lands?

Thinks about this with a pause

JIT: That is not so good.

Pause

JIT: Question.

Ques: Is there anything specific that I, as a lightworker, need to do to assist you more?

JIT: Everything is as it should be; you do not need to think; we will show you.

Voice is fading

JIT: Question.

Ques: Is there anything else we should know?

Ques: At this moment in time?

Very quietly spoken

JIT: No.

JAN: I can't open my eyes as I rise but not fully.

Ques suggests Jan comes back

JAN: Just one more, I know there is someone who wants to speak.

Jan asks if Ques is ok to stay for this.

JAN: I have a sense that someone or something is working on my stomach; there are sensations and like a circle surrounding my stomach area, pressure is felt and… (Healing.)

Jan goes deeper

Voice fades

A long pause while she goes into the altered state

JIT: Inform people of ways to help themselves. Inform the people of how it can be done.

Voice is raised towards the end of paragraph

JIT: Traces of their yester-years are no longer to be held onto. Traces of the moments before the time of now are no longer to be held on to. Traces of the moments that we feel in our hearts are no long to be held on to. Traces of the moments before the time, before the time, before the time, are no longer to be held on to.

JIT: Traces of the moments are just moments.

Quietly spoken

JIT: Traces of the moments.

Voice fluctuates between very quiet and loud

JIT: I shake my head and let go of the skin that surrounds my physique. I do not need that skin; I shed it now.

JIT: Move forward now. Move forward and walk this way. Use your mind to take you where you need to be; use your mind to help you with your earthly living.

JIT: Use your mind.

JIT: Check mate.

Continues with a different energy speaking

JIT: Come with me and I will show you. We go here; look.

JIT: Right, let us walk this way. You can hover if you want; let's go.

JIT: Close your eyes and let it be.

JIT: I will give out more information, later.

JIT: Crying is not the way forward; release those old patterns and let them be gone forever more.

JIT: Play the game, play the game.

JIT: One square at a time, I ask you to play the game.

Long pause

JIT: Release that kundalini, working with the kundalini.

Exhales

JIT: They will help you now, the lions and the tigers as they roar; they will lead the way, you will lead the way now. I will lead the way; you will lead the way.

Short pause.

JIT: Diamonds and pearls inside the crustaceans; they will give you the meaning of life...

Sighs as if to say that is all there is to the meaning of life.

JIT: It is all virtual. It is all the virtual reality. Let me take you there and show you; I let you go there.

Very slowly spoken and precise

JIT: I will take you to the room, here you can see anything. All the information you require to go forward in your earthly existence. Later I will show you this.

Preaches

JIT: You are bound by the earthly ties, release the earthly ties and allow thyself to flow forward. Flow into the maze and the checkerboards.

JIT: Flow into the maze.

JIT: Speak to me and it will be done.

JIT: Look at me and I will show you.

Pause

Ques: Who are you?

JIT: The voice.

JAN:

There was so much information in this dialogue and new experiences for me. To have the feeling of coming out but knowing I needed to go back down into trance, the rise and fall was such a pleasure. I felt they were closely connected to me. Almost in control.

Lots of hints on how we should be living our lives fully, to our highest potential. There is a room in the universe that we, as earthlings, can connect to that will enable us to potentially live our lives on earth with more direction and knowing.

Ques repeated questions previously asked and had answers to some new ones. There was a sense of agitation around some of the questions; the voice seemed to be annoyed at one point.

Ques seemed intent on asking for labels. Throughout *Zoetic Soul* you will have noticed that, except on the odd occasion, no such labels have been given or agreed. Although, you could use others' interpretation of scenes described, perhaps.

Should we label ourselves? Does this restrict us? What do you think?

I thank so many voices for enabling this session.

■ ■ ■

Jan Mayfield

10 Trance

03-Feb-2016

Present in the room

JIT: Jan in trance

JAN: Jan as Jan

Ques: Asking the questions

Jan makes herself comfortable again laying on the healing couch and begins to take herself into altered trance state for this connection to channel their voice.

JAN: The room feels different today, a different energy release and a deeper connected feeling.

JIT: Look at that clench in your belly; when it is time to release, breathe deeply.

JIT: Half past three.

Very deep altered state, breathless and anxious

JIT: Look at the quarter of the clock; when it says half past three, the time is coming. Feel that abrasive clench in your belly when you know it is time to release.

JIT: Feel that releasing beginning to happen as we do our work here on earth. As we do our work, feel that releasing beginning to happen. We will tell you and show you. Never be worried by the half past three.

JIT: There is always more. There is always something else. There are always the dreams that you need to follow. The dreams that you need to analyse with your earthly minds. Let the dreams flow and let the distance be shorter than it was before.

Deep breathing and out of breath panting

JIT: Transmutation moving forward, dynamite and diversity *breathless... making noises.*

Breathes heavy and is a little agitated

JIT: You don't have to do it when you are asleep. You have to do it now. Stay awake and let me do it; stay awake.

Breathes deep with a long exhale

JIT: One malfunction is being retrieved. All malfunctions are being retrieved.

Spoken in one breath

JIT: Trespass on the grounds, in the grounds, around the grounds you are not supposed to go. Trespass on those grounds; you will be shown that is not the way. You do not want to take the consequences if you trespass on the grounds where you are not supposed to go.

Ques: What grounds?

JIT: Where you are not supposed to go.

Ques: Where are they?

JIT: All around.

JIT: Walk through the fields with the horses; look to the ground and don't look up, you will see and you will find. You will be shown.

Deep breathing, pausing for a while

JIT: Each one has control now. I can see the four of us sitting in front of our screens looking down on you earthlings. We are four. We watch. We are the teachers; we will show you we are here to divinely guide you.

JIT: Red crusted rockets will fail; the engines will fail, and fall out of the sky.

JIT: Canada's grids will fail; there will be a power overload and the grids will come tumbling down. Look out for this day; things will change.

JIT: Jerusalem and Bethlehem, more truces will be opened; more doors will be opened, more will be closed too.

JIT: I will show you Jerusalem and Bethlehem; they are different to what the history books write.

Long pause, quiet voice

JIT: Monday, Tuesday, Wednesday.

JIT: We have control on Monday, Tuesday, Wednesday.

JIT: Thursday is freedom and Friday is Friday freedom.

JIT: Monday, Tuesday, Wednesday.

Ques: What was on Friday?

JIT: Freedom!

JIT: I will take questions.

Ques: You will take questions?

Ques: Have you got any future predictions for people to be aware of?

JIT: Look at the devaluations of money, see the monetary values rise and fall. Coins will disappear eventually.

JIT: 2026 is a big change.

JIT: The iron railing on the bridge over the water will collapse. The bridge over the city's water will collapse in line with the vessel.

Ques: Which city?

JIT: London.

Ques: What about the animals on earth?

JIT: Those that need to will survive; extinction is evolution.

JIT: 2018 shows more ice disappearing from the earth. The waters will swell one more time after the ice falls. They will swell and fall below that which has never been known before.

JIT: Christ mass is not; Christ mass will cease.

JIT: Japanese business people will be revealed with their plans for earth; they will be revealed in the nick of time.

JIT: America will lose the boundaries and will become one and be renamed.

Ques: What will it be renamed?

JIT: That is not for you to know yet.

JIT: Pluto and Jupiter will realign with earth, and when this happens it will show you the cross section that will reveal evidence of the future of the planet.

JIT: There is a baby being born and talked about with 4 ears.

Ques: I see.

JIT: I see others strange to you, oddities in births. In the future I see these happening around us.

Ques: Like the Zika virus in Brazil?

JIT: No.

JIT: This is different, simpler; there will be many things said about the child. The child will live and go on to be of the supernatural, but with earthly tendencies.

Ques: Do me and Jan need to visit any specific sites?

JIT: Sites?

Ques: Before we have been told to visit sacred sites?

JIT: You will be guided as to which ones to go to.

JIT: You will be guided.

Ques: Is there something that Jan and I need to do together?

JIT: You may go together.

JIT: I will show you.

Ques: Are you still working on us at night?

JIT: Yes, my child.

Ques: Is it in the stomach area?

JIT: All over.

Ques: Is this the psychedelic visions I keep getting?

JIT: What is psychedelic?

Ques: Multi coloured, strange, I can see light in a tunnel... hard to describe.

JIT ignores the question

JIT: There will be a blind person; who will have lots of information to carry into the future.

JIT: Look out for the blind person.

Ques: On the earthly plane?

Ques: Will we meet them here?

JIT: Yes.

Ques: So who is the blind person?

Chooses not to answer the question

Very long pause

Ques: Are you still there or gone?

Ques: Do you want more questions?

JIT: Yes.

Ques: You cannot reveal who the blind person is to us?

JIT: No.

Ques: Who are the four who look down to earth through the screen?

JIT: We are the four who work through the screens; we meet until the work is done. Until the work is done on the people, to give them the extra senses to enable them to move on in their lives on earth. Also, they will help us; they will give freedom and movement to the people in the country.

Ques: Are you working with other people as well as me and Jan?

JIT: No, other people I work with in the room.

Ques: All four of you work in this room.

Exhales fade

JIT: Yes!

Stronger voice

JIT: Temple Street. Friar Gate.

JIT: There will be victims of violence.

Ques: Why me and why Jan?

JIT: It is why you are here. Simple.

JIT: 329; number 329.

Ques: What is the significance of that?

JIT: You will see it is for future reference.

JIT: The ship in the harbour. The big ship in the harbour, the liner will have a malfunction underneath; water will enter from below. Future.

JIT: Deliberate actions are done to create this malfunction.

JIT: People will be running from the gyros in the country of Greece; they will run, they will flee from the cities to the small towns and villages and they will become their cities.

JIT: Gas.

JIT: The orange caves on another land will have more revealed than has been in the past. The orange caves.

JIT: August 19th, July 4th and April 27th we will be working towards these dates.

Ques: What year?

JIT: This year

Ques: 2016?

JIT: Correct.

JIT: Question.

Ques: There is an awful lot of information for us to digest, is it not, for us earthly beings?

JIT: It needs to be the written word for reference and reading... to be shared with the people and to be given out to the people. You will know when the time is right, collect all the information now and collate it all together.

Ques: Do we need to write a book and publish it?

Jan knew this is what she was doing, not sure why this question was asked.

JIT: Yes.

JIT: Jan has all the instructions; she knows what to do.

JIT: She has been guided to this for many years.

JIT: She will succeed, she will survive, she will pass all the information to all the people who need to read and hear it.

Ques: And what is my job... role?

JIT: As you are.

Ques: And what am I?

JIT: You are a lightworker.

Ques: I don't always understand my role as a lightworker.

JIT: You will have many changes to come. You have many things to work on and release. You will **then** understand your role. The time is not right; preparation is the key.

Ques: Are there many lightworkers?

JIT: Thousands.

JIT: In the world on earth, thousands.

Ques: Do they all have a vital role?

JIT: Yes.

Ques: Are the lightworkers' collective?

Fading

JIT: Yes. You are repeating questions.

JIT: My work is done now; I am closing the room with the four screens. The room is closing.

Ques: Thank you.

Long pause

JIT: Are your feet on the floor?

Ques: One is.

JIT: I need two feet on the floor.

Ques: Is there anything else you want me to do?

JIT: Silence is good.

Spoken very quietly

JIT: It is done.

Ques: What is done?

JIT: My work on that is done, I can go now.

Ques: Work on me or Jan?

Ignores the question

Very long pause – can hear mumbles

JIT: Teach the children to use their minds to walk up the beautiful paths, to the gardens, and find the open door in the right hand corner of the garden.

JIT: Teach the children to go and stand in the room. The children are everyone; teach them to go and stand.

JIT: The room is full of sweets, jarred sweets. Each sweet represents part of their lives; each colour represents the emotional feeling to do with that part of their life. The fullness of the jar represents the time spent in that period of time in that life.

JIT: Teach them to look at the jars, which are not full. They represent the lessons to learn and experiences to have. Look at the jars and see what description is on the label. This describes the lessons to be learned to fill the jar. When all the jars are full, incarnations are finished.

JIT: Simplified.

JIT: One can also go to the jars that are full or half full and ask to have those skills given to them in this life now. Anything that is learned before, anything that has been done before can be taken out of the jars and brought to this life on earth and used presently.

Pauses

JIT: This way if you are having problems in your life, you can find the emotion and the experience in one of the jars. As you have already completed this in a previous life, you can bring it through to help you.

JIT: Sometimes emotions and situations are jumbled up together and you cannot see, as you say, 'you cannot see the wood for the trees.' You cannot see this. Therefore visiting the room and taking what you have already learned will help you to see more clearly.

Spoken in a robotic way

JIT: I see you need liquorice and I see you need the black and white stripy sweets, and I see you need the ones in red paper with the cherries on it. Visit this place when you have the time.

Ques: Who, me?

JIT: Yes.

Ques: In meditation?

JIT: Yes.

JIT: Follow the garden route as described above.

JIT: You have five visits.

Ques: Do I need to do this five times?

JIT: You have five visits.

Ques: Can Jan take me to this place?

JIT: You can go yourself.

JAN:

As I was in the silence, I was working on Ques, working on her insides, makeup and soul. This was a very intense feeling. I was also taken to other people and the same was being done. I did not verbalise this. Only recalling the information as I transcribe the recording.

The garden and sweet shop scenarios are good to follow and will be created into a meditation.

Ques has been given some wonderful healing and alignment and so many indications of how to self-help in life. Everyone must want to change to enable change to flow. To be open minded and think beyond what someone else has taught you.

■ ■ ■

11 Trance

05-Feb-2016

Present in the room

JIT: Jan in trance

JAN: Jan as Jan

Ques: Asking the questions

Jan makes herself comfortable and begins to take herself into her altered trance state for this connection to channel their voice.

A very soft voice

JAN: This session begins with the feeling of intense heat but it is light brightness heat, not fire.

JAN: As I move along a pathway, I can see things appearing and disappearing on both sides. The rooms or places appear and then they go; I am walking up the path, but I am not walking.

This is as she goes into her altered state through her mind's eye

JIT: Moving forward it feels...

Very quiet, slow voice

JIT: Pausing by a space somewhere, there is a door. I am told to go in the door and check out the quantum leap, (Definition of quantum leap in the English dictionary: **A great improvement or important advance in something**) to show that anyone can go in here and help themselves.

JIT: I am going inside the room. There is everything you could ever want to connect to yourself.

JIT: So, if you wanted to be an artist, writer, educator, teacher or anything else. Enter the room and ask for yourself in a previous life. For example, to show yourself as the teacher. A film of you as the teacher is on the screen; you watch it and the skills and knowledge transfer to you. Skills required will be transferred to this life. You can ask for it to be played quickly.

JIT: You are looking as an outsider at the film; you observed the teacher, you, as the teacher. To know how it feels to be a teacher.

JIT: Coming out of that space.

JIT: Thank you.

JIT: I know now that I have the skills to become a teacher, an educator or someone giving guidance because I have been, and I picked the skills and brought them to the foreground of my memory. I will be able to do this now.

Very slowly spoken.

Pause.

JIT: On the other side is a semi-circle of people with one person in front of them; I can't see what they are doing. Anyway, they are taking me further forward in the space, I am moving forward. Anybody can access that room.

JIT: Further forward.

JIT: Flashes of rooms either side of me. Further forward I keep going.

JIT: Feels like I am going into a cave. Another space opens up to the left.

Breathes to move deeper into altered state

(I become the Orbie to experience this from their perspective.)

JIT: I am going in this one to sit on the chair in the middle of the room. In here, I see four walls and around the edges are arms with suckers on the ends. The suckers attach to the Orbie. They seem to choose which suckers they want and a flexible pipe connects to you as you sit in the chair. The room and the pipe know what you need. You can visit whenever you want. This is for Orbies. Not earthlings.

JIT: Information comes out of the wall to the Orbie, and some suckers take out information as you no longer need it.

JIT: It is a strange feeling, as though I am not me. I am being programmed for the future.

JIT: I can see different dimensions. I can see Pluto and other planets, and I can see different buildings/hologram rooms on and around the planets. In the stratosphere and the atmosphere there is a different layer where others appear; there are a whole set of different beings living there.

JIT: Someone just came and looked at me, an earthling wearing blue jeans and a beige/grey jumper that's hand knitted. I can see their face; they looked down at me. Male, darkish hair, earthly body. Popped in and out.

Said quickly

JIT: As I am looking forward to the right, I can see four habitations but the four don't intermingle and are millions of light years away from each other. They are showing me the different areas where *beings* were recently living; they all have their own agenda, and they all live in the way that suits the planet.

Long pause

Spoken with haste

JIT: It is important that people understand their potential ability to change the course of their own life at any given point.

JIT: It is important for them to understand that by using the different tools talked about, they can change their course.

JIT: By changing their perception of life they can learn to live in the moment. This will not stop them from planning for the future but it means that they are not using the emotion connected to earthly people that will cause them worry for the future.

JIT: They will live in the moment and know that everything will be right for them. As they reach the next moment, which will be that moment in time, there is only that moment in time. The moment that is now. You are doing this now because you are doing this now.

JIT: These people evolve, these people have confidence issues, they have self-belief issues, and they have fear and doubt. All these labels are attached to them for them to take off.

JIT: Let go to enable the freedom to live in that present moment. Far too many look at the soul's purpose. Looking for the soul's purpose will not give you the purpose. Living in the moment will create it.

JIT: Amazing happiness, a knowing feeling that everything for them at that moment in time is right. You will smile for no reason. We all strive to be in that place.

JIT: Questions.

Ques: How do we access that room at any time to change?

JIT: Repeat.

Ques: How do we access that room at any time to change?

JIT: Quantum leap, meditation.

Ques: Is this something that needs to be learned?

JIT: Meditation will take you to that place; ask and you will be given.

Long pause

Ques: Is this something we need to teach people?

JIT: Meditation will be taught to the people, yes.

Ques: Is this something that Jan needs to do?

Strong voice

JIT: Meditation, she does.

Ques: Yes, but does she need to teach meditation to people?

JAN: I do teach it to people. Ques did not know this.

JIT: Awareness, raising awareness.

Pause

Ques: What else do we need to know?

JIT: Later, you will be given that information.

Pause

Ques: Do we need to make people aware of the tools that are available?

Ques: To help them change and live in the moment, the time for now?

JIT: Yes.

Ques: So we need to start meditation groups then?

Pause

JIT: Raising awareness is key.

Ques: And what is the best way to do that?

JIT: All ways; everyone will receive information uniquely, so find different approaches to help the people to sort out their way forward. We will show you.

Breathes deep; goes deeper

Ques: Thank you.

Ques: It is difficult to know which questions I need to ask.

Moves on

JIT: Moving forward now to the future, moving forward in the times when earth will be changed; we are moving forward now. As I walk in the water.

Breathes

Upbeat and light

A different energy speaks

JIT: I feel the most amazing blue village, crystalized shapes.

JIT: Crystalized turrets, Crystalized shapes, Crystalized blue clear, Crystalized walkways.

JIT: So much beauty surrounds.

JIT: So much beauty guides the people to the bottom of the ocean which will then be revealed in the future.

JIT: Altars and seating in special rooms that have been locked for many thousands of years will be opened for others to see. People who have meditated before will have accessed different places.

JIT: They will no longer hold the keys to do this; they will be stripped of all their keys of entry. New people will receive the keys. New people will receive the access codes and vibrations to the underwater cities revealed. The long corridor in the crystal palace with all the doors locked will be opened for the people.

JIT: As we go through and look, there are three on the left and four on the right. Changes will happen on earth if these codes and keys are accessed by the people. There will be new comments for everyone to see; not all will want to, but it will be there for the chosen few.

JIT: Looking to go into the room asking for access. Access denied.

Ques: Which room?

JIT: Repeat.

JIT: All the rooms along the corridor are locked; it is not time yet.

There is a long pause

JIT: I am back into the black.

JIT: For all those that choose the right path. As the earth changes know there will be many different places for you to exist. Everything will be revealed; there will be many places that you can transport yourself to. Know that you will visit these places and then go back to what you call *home*. There will be numerous journeys made. All the space will be accessible for the majority of the people to activate; activation is the key.

Robotic words

JIT: Power and activation. Power is in the activation.

Ques: And how do you get the power?

JIT: The power?

JIT: It will be revealed.

Voice fades

JIT: Plenty of people on earth. Enough is said to show and give guidance for the future of your life to come, and on earth as it is now. Guidance is written for you to access. Learn how to access and you will survive.

Jan returns but cannot open her eyes; she moves deeper into her altered state

Pausing for a while

Exhales take her deeper

Recites the following

JIT: More third eye activations will take place over the coming time. More third eye activations will be released and opened; allow for the activations. The people will be ready for their activations.

JIT: This is very important. For them to move forward in the correct way they will need their third eye activated further.

A very robotic voice continues

JIT: Third eye activation is key.

JIT: There will be contamination in the milk of the cows on the farms. There will be contaminated milk. Dairy free.

JIT: Your body is power; learn how to use the power within. The power will activate all the codes and give you access to areas otherwise out of bounds. You either go forward with activation or you stay where you are or you fall by the wayside. That is life; that will be life.

JIT: Activate your bodies.

JIT: Learn how to use your chakras to enable you to further develop all areas in your body.

JIT: Learn all about your chakras; what do they like and what don't they like?

JIT: Learn all about your chakras.

JIT: Learn about energy flow.

JIT: Learn about the flow of energy.

JIT: Learn about the flow of energy; stagnant energy will not give you access and power to the areas needed.

JIT: Your body is power; your mind is power. Think of chakras, not organs, in your body. Work to make the chakra function to the highest possible frequency that can be.

JIT: Activate the third eye even further.

JIT: Seven doors are opened; seven doors representing a chakra. Each door represents a particular chakra. Walk along the path and walk past the doors, if your chakra is completely balanced and working on the right frequency, the door will be accessible. Only when each door has been opened, will you gain access to the further truths that be.

Robotic voice continues

JIT: One, two, three, four, five, six, seven chakra doors opened…

JIT: The doors for Jan are reactivated as she has been activated here before.

JIT: All will be revealed, that lies within the areas behind the doors. The information to be passed to the people on earth.

JIT: The place to reach is spherical, it is bright, it is the all-knowing all seeing place to be; once the doors are opened, access will be given.

Spoken quietly

JIT: Thank you.

Deep breaths to connect further robotic voice

JIT: There will be teachers on earth who will enable not only the alignment of chakras, but activate access to open the door frequencies. This important process will become widespread.

JIT: Add this to your tools.

Quiet voice mumbles

JIT: Thank you.

A different Orbie energy speaks

JIT: The species of the sea will become abundant and vast; there is food in the water which can be eaten.

JIT: Sweden and Norway will have the abundant seas and also droughts.

JIT: Educate the people, bring all the tools together and show them the way.

JIT: Questions.

Ques: What is the best way to activate the chakras?

JIT: Meditation, diet, food, drink, colour, belief, faith, healing, balance, knowing and in the moment.

JIT: Next.

Ques: The best food, is it dairy-free?

JIT: Yes.

Long pause and waits

Ques: And third eye activation, is that through the pineal gland?

JIT: This has a bearing, but not only this.

Ques: What else?

JIT: It will be given to the people when the time is right. The people will know. The people will understand. This is not for everyone.

Breathes to take deeper

Ques: Does the crystal palace under the sea have a name?

JIT: No, no earthly name.

Ques: Are there any more projections for the future we need to know about now?

JIT: No more.

Long pause

Ques: Is the tool box complete now?

JIT: Other information to complete the toolbox will be given when it is necessary for the people to understand the other tools.

JIT: Thank you.

JAN:

This was one of the most uplifting sessions. Even as I transcribed it, I am lifted and have a euphoric feeling.

I can do this. I want this. Show me how. I can hear people saying this as they feel like I do.

I have entered the rooms before and I do smile for no reason. I live my soul's purpose. We are giving you the tools to do this. The tools will be correlated for easy access and flow.

The way it is suggested to look at the chakras instead of the organs in the body, each chakra does represent so much within our bodies.

■ ■ ■

Sessions 12-15

Trancing takes a different turn, as Jan works with her inner guide, she allows guidance to be mindful.

Visions that reveal confirmations that we can change and we can live our **Soul's Purpose**.

Jan receives healing, and further confirmations that all areas of the universe may be mindfully accessed.

12 Trance

08-Feb-2016

Present in the room

JIT: Jan in trance

JAN: Jan as Jan

Thought Voice: Jan thinking words as a human

Ques: Asking the questions

Jan makes herself comfortable and begins to take herself into her altered trance state for this connection to channel their voice.

JAN: Today there is a strange sense that no one is around. I am uneasy and not entering trance. The usual signs had not arrived and I had an overwhelming urge to manoeuvre into a foetal position, instead of lying on my back. As I took up this position, within seconds I was in altered state.

A beautiful, upbeat voice

JIT: Peter Pan of Never-Never land. Who wants to grow up anyway, what does it mean?

JIT: Ask yourself thousands of questions, the meaning of life and the meaning of this and the meaning of that. You never really get the answers.

JIT: Why don't you all just live, why don't you live like now, and stop looking for the answers to different things?

JIT: Live and be mindful, give your minds to me.

Ques: And who are you?

JIT: Mindful, I am mindful; give your minds to me and I will show you everything that you need to know about it.

JIT: IT is the all-encompassing everything. **IT** has many forms. **IT** is this, **IT** is that. (IT-Intelligent Transference.)

Pause

JIT: We sow the seeds in your mind for them to germinate and grow. We sow the seeds for you to fertilise. For you not to kill with the weed-killer, for you not to douse with all that water, for you not to finish off. We sow the seeds for them to grow into the most beautiful flowers. In your heads. In your garden heads. Only some of you will **allow** them to germinate and **bloom** to the most beautiful flowers you have ever seen. Open your mind to the possibilities, open your mind to the functions.

JIT: Give us grace.

JIT: Charcoal.

JIT: Look also for the other natural materials that will aid and be used in the future of life. Charcoal is the burner.

JIT: Look up, my dear children, at the properties of the tomato pip. What else can a tomato pip be used for? What is it and why do you take it into your diets? Why do you eat it?

JIT: Be mindful of why you eat all these things. Why you consume the foods you do. Stand with me at the bottom of the step, stand with me in your mind. Let me take you. Let me hold your hand and we can walk together.

Pausing - giving

JIT: Just stand with me and look, look at the beautiful dark. We see the steps are asking to form in front of you.

JIT: We are going to walk up the steps.

JIT: Four of them.

JIT: One, two, three, four.

JIT: And now the steps go down.

JIT: We will go down.

Slowly

JIT: One, two, three, four, five, six, seven, eight, nine, ten.

JIT: As you reach step ten, I want you to put your hand on your heart. Put it there, on your heart, and ask to be shown whatever you need to know.

JIT: Ask for whatever you need to know. Ask to be shown whatever is right for you today.

JIT: With your hand on your heart just look forward and I am asking the room to come to us.

Different voice - this is called thought voice

Spoken at speed- it is the jumbled human mind

Thought Voice: I don't know what to ask for, what should I ask for? Oh goodness what should I ask for, he has asked me to put my hand on my heart. Now what do I ask for? Do I need to ask? Or shall I just wait and see? Just wait and see I think.

Back to the other voice

JIT: Out of the black is a room coming closer towards me. Stopping, and showing me the door to enter through. When I open the door, I can go inside and I see a chair in the centre.

JIT: I go and sit on the chair.

JIT: I look all around the walls.

JIT: I can't really see anything; they are walls, but not walls.

JIT: There are some sort of metal structures inside the room.

JIT: It is beginning to show itself.

JIT: In front of me is a big shelf being constructed… appearing.

JIT: Just me in the room and my friend outside the door.

Ques: Who is your friend at the door?

JIT: The one who brought me here.

JIT: So a big shelf is constructing itself in front of me and there is a screen starting to open up. I am sitting on the chair. As the screen opens, I feel like it is looking at me but I can't see anything.

JIT: Oh, there is a big eye appearing on the screen now, so it looks at me.

JIT: It is connecting to my forehead.

Ques: Third eye?

Question ignored

JIT: I am being shown the library; the knowledge is being given to me through my forehead.

JIT: I am also being given déjà vu moments from my past- things that have happened to me in the past that I need to recall. These are not memories or things that have finished. They were unfinished and are meant to be coming back into the future.

JIT: I am being shown these moments. They will appear in front of me. In front of me in my life when I my life reaches that time.

Voice changes again

Thought Voice: I feel a bit mixed up. I don't know what is going on, if the truth be known.

Thought Voice: I am just sitting here feeling all different sensations in my body and I feel that I know what I am doing is right.

Pause

Jumps in with

Thought Voice: They are telling me that there is a forked-tongued person around, a snake-like person who is talking about you and will talk about things that you do.

Moves on; thought voice: ends

JIT: I feel very calm and very peaceful as my mind is being worked on.

JIT: As I come out of there, I see that someone else is waiting, I stand back and let them go in.

Ques: Who is the forked-tongued person?

Question is ignored

JIT: That one goes in and sits on the chair. I watch through the door and they are asking for advancements in their life. Things to make them move forward, things to help them in their life. They are not being very specific, just asking for advancements.

JIT: The eye is a little different as it comes on the screen for the next person, the principles are the same.

JIT: We watch for a while, then leave.

JIT: The eye on the screen connects to the person; it gives them knowledge and mind tools for the future.

JIT: Their futures and all turn...

Was about to say something then changed direction

JIT: I will take you now, wait; all stand in line and wait for me.

JIT: Up the steps.

JIT: Ten nine seven six five three one.

JIT: Four three two one.

A very long pause it taken

Slowly spoken

JIT: Everyone will be programed to see things more clearly; babies, adults, all genders. There will be more helpers beamed down out of the clouds.

JIT: They will be seen but not believed.

Spoken in very slow speech in one breath

JIT: 232 "A" squared minus the deliverance plus the ratio of the sum of the 27th arc in the auric field 19 4 3 to the power of 6 pi r squared plus the square root of 4252 dimensionalised the frequency of the radio waves in the Outer Hebrides.

Long pause

JIT: Must turn the papers upside down to read the writing in a different way, turn the papers upside down. There will be a key.

Sounds fun and light hearted

JIT: Topsy Turvy and melodramatic.

JIT: That is what I hear.

Slow speech

JIT: Another ancient pyramid will be revealed. Sand storms will reveal the top and it will be dug out; the sand will be moved from around it and it will be dug out.

JIT: Two Greek islands will crash and fall into the sea, leaving a fraction of the land space.

JIT: Connecting New Zealand and rugby and an amazing player being called bionic.

JIT: 2027 sees the children in the schools being sent home very upset and crying. The parents collect them. They come out of the schools crying.

Ques: Why?

JIT: Crying and sad. Something has happened in the world, I don't know why.

Long pause

JIT: Secrets will be revealed in the old opera house.

Speaks to self

Mumbles

JIT: The building of the foreign churches will be blasted; religion is no more. The books that are read from the ancient times all become one as we move forward.

JIT: New fabrics will be created and they will be a second skin.

JIT: So close to nature, they will have healing properties built into them and there holds another key.

JIT: Stimulation on the third vertebrae. Power points from healers will activate the brain stem. Healers, please be guided by us to deliver the healing needed to the universe. Be mindful of the healing that it is under the guise of many different names; be mindful of the healing, the universal energy healing. It is all one.

JIT: It does not need to be reproduced under different names. We have the name, now please believe we will guide you, the healers, to produce and make changes in the bodies of the people. Also, to enable them to heal themselves, more people will be spiritually aware and guided for themselves. Listen for yourself and believe what we say. And you will live your soul's purpose.

Chirps in

JIT: Do you know how crepe paper is made?

JAN:

As I transcribe this I am taken in my mind to the actual trance session, this is such a meaningful dialogue with so many indicators for you to use in your life which will enable the happiness within.

Meditation once again shows to be key for us to enable forward thinking and movement.

We were shown that we can access all areas. Is this the key to **Soul Purpose** living?

■ ■ ■

13 Trance

10-Feb-2016

Present in the room

JIT: Jan in trance

JAN: Jan as Jan

Ques: Asking the questions

Jan makes herself comfortable and begins to take herself into her altered trance state for this connection to channel their voice.

JAN: I am aware that as I relax the spirits are performing healing on my body, especially in my abdomen area.

JIT: It will be a trilogy.

Ques: What will?

Ignored the question

JIT: We are all sitting down, we are all lining up, we are all waiting.

JIT: We can have questions now.

Ques: What will be the trilogy?

JIT: Trilogy? Why do you speak of the trilogy? We do not understand.

Ques: Just now someone said this... what trilogy?

JIT: We are not aware of that.

QUES: So have you lived on earth before as a human?

JIT: I?

Ques: Or all of you?

JIT: Yes, we have lived on the planet of earth in the vehicle of a body.

Ques: And what was your purpose?

JIT: On earth?

Ques: Yes.

JIT: To live my life, we all came to earth to live our lives. To live in the now and move forward. Move forward in that moment of time that is now. Ever evolving, moving forward now.

Jan exhales deeper

JIT: The purpose is doing what you are doing; the purpose is doing the job that isn't the job. That is the purpose, enjoyment, fulfilment.

Ques: Where are you now? What dimension are you in now?

JIT: I don't understand the question. What are you asking?

JIT: We are in the space. We are in what we describe to you as the black, we are in the space.

JIT: We live as you would say beyond, the beyond, and we live beyond. We travel and we move. They bring to us anything that we need; anything we need is ours to use. We are not only dedicated to the place where we are now. We can move and be where we wish to be; evolution, my dear one.

Waiting for the next question

Ques: Do people need to know this? Know about dimensions and the black, where you are?

JIT: As we have said before, people should be understanding of the fact that they can access anything they want to at any given time.

JIT: Is that what you call knowing about this?

Ques: Sort of… but as you know, earthly beings relate to dimensions and parallel universes. Which is why I asked if the black has a name.

JIT: We don't have a name for the black. This is how it is seen; the universe, we can call it, or black.

This person seems to be talking about it as a whole not broken down into different areas

JIT: Everything can be accessed from anywhere; you just need to know how to do it. Believe and trust that we can show you. If you do not believe and trust this, then you will be forever looking for something and you will be looking forever.

We can move you through the walls and show you a time before and a time in the future and a time here and a time there. I can move you through different places and different avenues to show you. You need to live your earthly life now.

Breathes deeper into altered state

Ques: Is that our purpose as humans, to live this life and then go into the black to learn more?

Raised stern voice

JIT: You live now! Every minute of every day is now. So, you live in the now moment. You make learnings/experiences and you help people. You help with evolution.

I don't understand; why the purpose?
Present yourself to the now; learn how to access all the information and this is how earthly lives should be. When you come to earth, when you are born to

earth, you are given a set of tasks, experiences and learnings. It is your perception of these; it is how you decide to work with these learnings that will determine your outcomes. If you choose to make things into big problems for yourselves then your outcomes will be big problems.

Should you choose to, you can deal with something in the way that you were supposed to deal with it in the first place. Allow ego and past emotions come into it and you will never get where you need to be going.

JIT: Set aside all the emotions and egos, and all the feelings that will hold you back. It is important to allow yourself to be free to go forward.

Pauses and deep breathes

Ques: What is the relevance of the third vertebrae, can you expand on that?

Pauses

JIT: It holds the key to releasing. This... *stops what he was going to say*

Pauses, waiting for the question

Ques: What is *this*?

JIT: This?

Ques: Releasing what?

Raised voice

JIT: Life on earth, becoming the person, becoming one, accessing all areas.

Ques: Do that with the chakras?

JIT: This helps.

Ques: And what else?

Ques: What else helps?

Questions are too quick

Said with speed and raised voice

JIT: We have spoken before about the vortexes, we have spoken before about the mind, and we have spoken about accessing areas. Areas not actually seen by the human eye. Therefore, we will be using our minds to access most of the areas.

You must trust and believe that we will come in and show the people the way they are supposed to be going. Once they have **released** it will allow their earthly bodies to be accessed.

Ques: Is there anything else you need us to know?

JIT: All messages are delivered at the time of importance.

JIT: All learnings are delivered at the time of importance.

Pauses

Waiting a while for the question

Silence

Ques: Is Mary with you?

JIT: Mary will be here later.

Ques: Are there any other questions I need to ask?

JIT: We have given you information that will enable you to live your earthly life in quite a peaceful way, and will allow for changes coming in.

JIT: We are not understanding of the question.

Deep breathes

Ques: When you say we, how many are there?

JIT: We here now today are five.

Ques: And do all five of you have a different purpose?

There is a long pause before answering

I feel agitation with this question about purpose...

JIT: Purpose?

JIT: I don't understand.

Ques: Different role, five different bits of information?

JIT: We are as one.

Mumbles and waits

And waits

Spoken fast, in a determined voice without breaths

JIT: The purpose of these sittings is to enable the people to understand that they can access all areas of the universe. They can access whatever they wish to, whatever information they choose to access. We are here to show the people this. They will understand that with a few tools they can access to make changes to their own lives.

As they live on earth, it will not only make changes to their lives but it will also enable them to move through problems. To move through controversy. To move through governments. To move through countries. To move through all areas and all aspects.

They now have all key information; you have it all!

JIT: Do you understand? Can you see the tools we have given you?

Ques: Who am I speaking to now?

Getting agitated

JIT: I am the voice of information.

Ques: Have we been given all the tools?

Abrupt

JIT: Yes.

Ques: And we now need to spread the word to the people, yes?

Spoken in a very robotic way with speed and no emotion

JIT: The people will know and understand.

Pause

JIT: Death should not be feared; death is just a movement from one place to another. From one thing to another, from one situation to another, death is the ending of one thing and the start of something else; death should not be feared.

JIT: Death is only feared because people allow their emotions to become a problem and they think they will never see that person again. However, if they believed they would see that person again; knowing they are evolving into a larger spirit. They would be happy for that person passing. Negative emotions should not come into transitioning.

Waits

Such a long pause here

JIT: Divine intervention will always be there; we are the divine, we will intervene.

Breathes deeper into altered state

Ques: Are you the same as what earthlings call angels?

JIT: No.

Ques: Do angels exist?

JIT: You have seen the angels, and we talk to the angels.

Ques: Do they help us as well?

JIT: Of course.

JIT: Do you not know you have angels that come around and help?

Ques: Yes, I do. A lot of people believe in angels.

JIT: Why then was the question asked? We will retire soon.

JIT: We will step back and allow you to do your work. We will step back and continue with ours; the information we have given will suffice until the next one.

Ques: Do we need to come together again?

JIT: We will call upon you.

Ques: So we cannot access you at any time?

JIT: We will speak to Jan; we communicate with her. She will receive the communication as is necessary.

Ques: Are other people doing the same work on earth as we are here?

JIT: Not the same work, no. There are people doing similar work in different areas on the earth. Everyone will be given information variables to suit the communities they live and work in. Those people who are given this information as Jan is, will be able to distribute to their chosen audience when the time is right.

JIT: We will give her extra protection now because of the forked tongues. We have spoken of the forked tongues before.

JIT: We will give protection and we will erase from sight.

Ques: Who are the forked tongues?

JIT: It is no matter.

Very long pause here

Jan exhales a few times; this takes her deeper into altered state

Said slowly

JIT now speaks as Mary

JIT: (Mary) Listening to the prayers and the poems and the stories that were read to me, all the words are coming into my mind. I could not move my body, I felt the healing, as it penetrated through my skin and bones and eased away the pain and tightness in my joints to my mind.

JIT: (Mary) I could see the people as they came into the room. I could read their thoughts as I moved from one dimension to the other. The passageways were clear to me. I lay for far too long waiting to be called. That time was there to create that bond of extra love and knowing; this was your learning *(Jan's learning)*. I was in the other dimension and did visit when you did.

JIT: (Mary) You will know that as one soul leaves the earthly body, it transports itself to the place where it revisits its life on earth. There were so many special times we had together. As I sit in front of the screen, I was shown everything from birth to transition; everything I did was correct and everything I said was correct. The century I gave to earth was correct.

Ques: Are you Mary?

JIT: I am Mary now.

JIT: (Mary) As I sit and watch the screen they talk to me about the earthly times, about the different opportunities and poignant moments just as they used to talk to me when I sat in the chair and closed my eyes. I was always guided by the ones just as you are, my dear.

JIT: (Mary) I guide you now from that day that I transitioned, I guide you.

JIT: (Mary) And as I speak, I tell you the words, everything I give you to think about is everything that you need to know. Everything that passes through your spirit brain, as you call it, is there for you. As you sat beside the bed with my carcass you held my hand and spoke words of wisdom, belief, trust and truth; we thank you for that. We now give back to you the same.

You are my child on earth, and I was your mother 1329.

Breathes deeper

JIT: (Mary) Never stop; continue as you are and you will understand more and more as it is given, relaying the information as you do when it is required.

JIT: (Mary) April is the target. September sees you moving out of your cave, September sees you being put in place with that dream we have given you so many times. September you will be there. Continue to self-talk in the present moment, continue to have that motivation and continue to listen to what I discuss with you.

JIT: (Mary) 924 I was your son. 1503 we were twins not to be born. There were many other times of which I do not need to speak now. Continue to allow Isaac to pen the paper. He will always be with you, as will I.

A short pause

JIT: (Mary) September 2016 is the time you ask about.

JIT: (Mary) January 2017 sees the travel.

JIT: (Mary) Money worries were eradicated many months before. The right time as you live in the moment, is the right time for you to love.

JIT: (Mary) There will be three passings in succession; those three will be before April 2017. You know. You know what you have to do, my dear child.

JIT: (Mary) I welcome you as I work to make everything right. Sometimes earthly events get in the way, but I work on you day and night.

JIT: (Mary) Set the goals and let me see. To have it on paper will be easier for you. Let Isaac and I take your hand as you write; the future will be yours, and you will be given the goals. The sanctuary will be yours, the sanctuary for the people.

JIT: (Mary) I am helping with the pain- just lay.

She gives wonderful healing to Jan

JAN: A very special feeling of overwhelming love and intense healing, like nothing from earth.

JIT: (Mary) Tennessee, Carolina, New Zealand and Australia.

JIT: (Mary) Look for the mirror that is set with pearls, look for the reflection.

Such a deep altered state

JIT: (Mary) The tree of knowledge and pick off what you would like. Access all areas; you have the key. Go now, my child, and continue. I will hold your hand forevermore.

JAN: That was so very beautiful and emotional to receive such a personal message from my Grannie Mary, words cannot thank you enough.

A very long pause and stillness

JAN:

As I emerge from this very special session, I can see a huge Peacock butterfly who has its wings open wide. The upper side of its wings are the most amazing shades of purple, turquoise and lemon with translucent white accents. Each corner of the wings has the most realistic eye.

All Seeing Eye...

Thank you Grannie Mary once again for being there for me in this lifetime and as you have stated here in past lives together. I did not know this.

This session has lots of information for you all to help you with your future and living in that wonderful place of now.

■ ■ ■

14 Trance

12-Feb/2016

Present in the room

JIT: Jan in trance

JAN: Jan as Jan

Ques: Asking the questions

Jan makes herself comfortable and begins to take herself into her altered trance state for this connection to channel their voice.

JAN: I can see a wedding dress! This could have a meaning of marriage/unity of something.

JAN: As I go further into trance, I am shown periods of my own life. Things that spirits have given me over the years are being brought to my attention. Spiritual work and mostly the not so normal earthly life events. I am being shown everything given to me over the years. I am unable to move deeper into trance. I have to watch the screen!

JAN: I recall the events and I am told not to discuss them in this recording. Spirit is making sure I can remember everything, perhaps to be used later in life.

Going deeper

JAN: I know someone is standing behind me with their hands on my head holding it still. I know I am receiving healing.

JAN: I am deeper now, but still not enough to trance a voice.

JAN: Someone is at my feet, and they are gripping my ankles. When I say someone, I mean it is a spirit energy!

JAN: It feels wonderful; I feel they are connecting me to some divine healing, forcing strange sensations to run though my body. The pressure on my stomach is strong and I can't feel my legs touching the couch. They are heavy and dead.

Jan is still and quiet for a while

JAN: I can feel so many different sensations. I just know it is healing.

All of a sudden the tranced voice speaks

JIT: Follow that train of thought, follow that train and know that as time goes by more will be given to you. Follow the ideas that we are putting in your head. Follow your thoughts that come from us.

JIT: There will be more spiders who will grow. A deadly species will be developed, even more deadly than the ones of now.

Ques: Will they be created by humans?

JIT: Natural evolution.

Ques: What is the purpose of bigger spiders?

JIT: There is no purpose. It just is.

JIT: Look for the binary fields; changing the binary codes will help. It will aid the conflicting figures of the mathematical calculations that can be seen. Changing the binary will have an effect not seen by man before.

JIT: Binary codes will change and binary codes will be no more.

A pause is taken

JIT: What do the Chinese do with all their hair?

Ques: I don't know?

JIT: Energy.

Ques: Like Goliath? When they cut his hair, he lost his strength.

JIT: No.

JIT: The hair that falls on the floor is scooped up and taken away to be used for energy.

JIT: We are connecting now to some of the lost souls.

JIT: Some of the lost souls are brought back together and put in their rightful place. There is peace on earth.

JIT: There will be more peace on earth; the peace comes from within to create the peace on earth. People choose not to be peaceful people. Out of all the teachings, out of all the voices that have spoken, the information we have given you, you must be able to see that the peace and the learning and the creation come from within.

Connect to the within and everything else will fall into place and **be**.

JIT: Yes, you will see the vibrations as they change; the objects as they become something different. You will see through the time zones. You will see as we have shown Jan the walls that are not walls. You will see through into the past or something that happened in the same place that you sit; she is to give her example here… she will know.

JAN: My example will be added at the end of this dialogue.

JIT: You must see that connecting to the inner self is allowing you to be the one that drives forward. The one that creates. The euphoric ambiance of living can only be found within. We do not talk of material things; we talk about, in earthly terms, the contentment, the satisfaction, the knowing, the confidence, the self-esteem. All those words are put in a bag and put inside you and melted down to become living in the moment.

JIT: There is no right or wrong way in the moment, because you are in that moment. So many gurus, educators and teachers have tried to impart this information to the world, and it is received by many. However, it needs to be brought into the 21st Century. To be used by the people as they live their lives from now forward; the information of the old is adapted to be delivered to the younger people… to the older people too as they can use this information to create that euphoric experience, before they take their transition from their earthly body.

JIT: Such amazement and awe is seen and felt. Everyone, the majority, should and can walk around in this state and just be. Having that knowing feeling that radiates the love without thinking about giving the love. It radiates the love naturally; there is no requirement to give out love in an earthly way. Being within and having that beautiful energy inside will radiate the love. This love is pure love.

JIT: This love is divine love; this love is the love that there is. Other people who live in the now and radiate this love will see it in their fellow people. Those who do not vibrate on that frequency will not see it as the love, because they are working from an earthly human experience. Let go and you will begin to radiate the love. The love needs and will radiate throughout the universe.

Pausing here

JIT: Connect to one's own self to feel the warmth. Cradle your mind in your own beautiful warmth of love.

Pause

JIT: Love divine loves all excelling. Love is divine and it does excel to the others that feel the same.

Pause. Gives a random piece of information

JIT: I want to give you blackberries freshly picked from the bushes.

Ques: Do you have a name?

JIT: The voice. I am the voice that speaks the necessary words to give you the information to pass on to the people. We just are.

JIT: We talk of the dimensions and we talk of the planets and you talk of the frequencies. We that are the voice just are. We bypass the frequencies; we bypass the dimensions and sit high and watch. Soon, as will be revealed that we can access all areas in our minds, we can access all areas. Vision is used to access. However, this is not for everyone; this will be used and shown to people on earth, as and when they need it. I am the voice that speaks of the universe.

Ques: Have you started to show me when I am sleeping?

JIT: Show?

Pause

Ques: Last night when I was sleeping, what was I shown?

Rather stern voice

JIT: Development will be taking place.

Ques: While I am sleeping?

JIT: All of the time.

JIT: Some of the information we give, some of the development we give is below and above your human radar. You will not connect to that frequency; you will just know that something is different or changed.

JIT: It is not yours to question, it is yours to accept.

JIT: This is not talking to you personally the one that questions. This is talking to the world, the universe. Anyone who reads this information will understand things can happen and vibrations can change. Moon cycles and many other things can alter, there is no earthly feeling you just know that something is different.

This is what we speak of, to give you the wonderful knowing feeling. That you are where you are and that you are where you are meant to be. If you Ques-tion you are not.

Long pause and deep exhales

A change of energy speaking through Jan

JIT: Two poles will split; there will be a divide, a crack, a change when the two polarities... this cannot be reversed. However, there will not be too many major changes with this happening.

Long pause

JIT: I wish to end there for today. I wish to tell you three times more I will come and speak. Three times more I will give you information. Listen to the work that is given before the next time that I visit, listen and develop.

Ques: Thank you.

JIT: Goodbye.

JAN: I can still sense someone holding my head, it feels wonderful with healing sensations, as I lay and drink in the energy given. I thank the spirits for what I have received.

WALLS THAT ARE NOT WALLS

JAN:

Early one morning, in a scenic town in Northern England, I was waiting for breakfast in the restaurant of a hotel. Shabby chic style decorated this elongated room with tables and chairs on either side; large windows filled the spaces on the left and bottom of the room. I sat at a table on the left-hand side and began to drink my tea. Hungry for my breakfast, I looked out of the window to my left. It viewed the outside which was a covered area for those who wanted to eat and drink in the fresh air. I remember hanging baskets full of beautiful flowers with petals of pinks and scattered with yellow.

I was aware that I had spirits with me. My usual signs were there. As I looked towards the outside, the wall beneath the window began to make a wavy motion. The solid was becoming more fluid. I watched to see what was going to happen, the window became fluid. I could not see the window and wall at this point. I was viewing a scene from The Edwardian Days. I determined this by the fashion. The colour and the flowers faded as the figures were shown to me.

I could see people, ladies, men and children dressed in costumes from that era. I blinked and looked away. I looked around to see who else might be gazing out of the window. The chatter between the couples in the restaurant was evident. No one else was looking that way. I watched for what seemed like a few minutes. The people looked towards me and I can still see one lady in my mind's eye. As our eyes met, she smiled as they all continued on their way. I was brought back by the waiter setting my breakfast on the table. As he walked away, I looked back at the window; the flowers and the colour had returned. I could not get back to the Edwardian scene.

I have on many occasions experienced the change in solidity of objects, I can look at objects and they will begin to change. How I do this? I really don't know. Clearly the spirits on the other side know and want me to share my experience here.

I am always humbled by the visions, sightings and conversations I have that are miraculously out of this world.

Ques was asking about herself and the voice told her that everything was for everyone. To be shared with the universe. This session and indeed other sessions, were not just about one person. Although I feel there was one session aimed at Ques giving her tools to enable future development.

■ ■ ■

15 Trance

02-March-2016

Present in the room

JIT: Jan in trance

JAN: Jan as Jan

JIT: (Mary) Jan in trance speaking as Grannie Mary

Ques: Asking the questions

Jan makes herself comfortable and begins to take herself into her altered trance state for this connection to channel their voice.

JAN: In this dialogue I am speaking as Grannie Mary. I had a message from spirit as I meditated before the session that she would be coming through.

JAN: I began to move into altered state and Grannie Mary was there. In everyday life she enters like this; one minute she is there and the next she is gone.

JIT: (Mary) Eliminating the barriers.

JIT: (Mary) In life we create our own barriers and we create our own blockages. We create walls and boundaries. Some are there for the good but others will stop you moving forward in your lives; you will need to let down the barriers.

The voice is high and uplifted

JIT: (Mary) Where are your goals?

JIT: (Mary) What goals do you have in life?

JIT: (Mary) You cannot do anything without your goals; get your little books out and write your goals down.

JIT: (Mary) What would you like?

JIT: (Mary) Where would you like to go?

JIT: (Mary) How would you like to do it?

JIT: (Mary) What would you like to see?

JIT: (Mary) Ultimately, what are your goals? You might never reach them but your journey will be fabulous, working your way towards them.

Get your little books out and write buzz words down. What buzz words do you like? Write your affirmations, go and get your little notebooks. Get a new one tomorrow.

Still upbeat

JIT: (Mary) Be happy, be vibrant, be buoyant and change the energies around you. Enable yourselves to be lifted, enable all the people of the world to be lifted.

Send out the love and feel the love coming back to you. Solitary love and self-love is just as good.

JIT: (Mary) Miles and miles apart we feel, but just a little millimetre away is where everyone else is standing. We are not that far apart; we are close together.

JIT: (Mary) We have all sorts, looking at this one and looking at that one. All they are doing is looking in the books that have been written before; stop looking in the books, all you people of the universe. Make up your own minds. Do not follow the books of the other people if you can help it.

JIT: (Mary) How the innocent will fall. It is no good hiding under that bush in the garden because that won't get you anywhere, will it? That is just another boundary. Cut your bush and let it all hang out and move forward with your life.

JIT laughs out loud here

So happy is the tone of her voice

JIT: (Mary) Move on forward, dance around, oh...

She loved to dance

...here we go round the mulberry bush, here we go round the mulberry bush, ha da da ta da *(She forgot the words.)*

JIT: (Mary) See how uplifted I am feeling now I am singing?

JIT: (Mary) You will bring the laughter and the songs to the people; you will bring your voice to the people.

JIT: (Mary) Joking aside, life can be as serious or a fun as you want to make it. To help people let go of their boundaries is a wonderful thing. This can happen; you can do this; you will show them.

Very stern now

JIT: (Mary) Hearts are pumping with fire; hearts are pumping with that red wonderful inky juice. Your heart is pumping with fire. So long as your heart is pumping you are alive in that earthly body to live the life you asked to come and live; do not forget this.

Pauses

JIT: (Mary) Target the younger ones that are beginning to open up, as they will be there for you to show them the way. Pass out the meditations, create the meditations.

Pauses

JIT: (Mary) Keep that excitement bubbling within your veins, keep that excitement racing around as you begin to look within yourselves. This will enable you to start to love yourselves. This is for the people of the universe because they who are teachers already understand my words; the other people of the universe you will need to look within. You should be releasing anything that will stop you going forward and anything that you do not love anymore.

JIT: (Mary) Peaches and cream.

JIT: (Mary) Custard Creams and Ginger Nuts.

(Those were her favourites biscuits dipped in very strong tea. After tea we would always have peaches and evaporated cream from the tin.)

Spoken at speed

JIT: (Mary) Look beyond what you can see, take your eyes out further afield from where you are looking at the moment. Keep looking, keep going, keep making all the countries join together; you are creating a spider web effect so keep joining the countries together. They will not come to you. You need to be spreading your web over the other countries.

JIT: (Mary) Listen to the symphonic orchestras as they play, listen as they resonate within your bellies, listen as they resonate throughout your body; find the music that resonates within your soul and feed your soul with the music.

JIT: (Mary) I like a cup of tea... *(She did, nice and strong was the only way.)*

Pause

JIT: (Mary) Steer clear of the purpose-built anything, steer clear of the additives and only have the fresh. Food, my dear children, only have the fresh foods.

JIT: (Mary) Do you have a question or two?

Ques: Do you have a question or do you want me to ask?

Long pause waiting for Ques. She asked you for a question

JIT: (Mary) Ready to start.

Ques: Should Jan do the book first then do the webinar?

JIT: (Mary) I don't understand.

Ques: Well, we have the book with the tools, and start of the webinar; should she do the book first?

JIT: (Mary) Yes, my child.

Ques: And what part do I play in all this? I don't feel as though I am doing enough.

JIT: (Mary) Part to play?

Ques: Yes, what part do I have to play?

JIT: (Mary) Everything is as it is, everything is correct. We are guiding you to be here today; this is the work that you should be doing and there are no changes to be made.

JIT: (Mary) All will be revealed and all will fall into place, if you think about the greater scheme of things. Always think about the bigger picture; this will always fall into place. We will always show you everything as it should be.

JIT: (Mary) Jan has been doing this work for many years and she has been building up to these moments in time; everything for her too will fall into place. I am showing her and I am showing you all the times ahead; you will have yours when the time is right. The visions will be there for you to see and act upon and make the choice as to whether you decide to go forward in that way.

Breathes deeper into her altered state

Pause

JIT: (Mary) If **we** wish to make any changes, we will make this happen.

JIT: (Mary) Everyone's abilities will be utilised and everyone has their own ability at any given time. We will not overload in a particular way.

Robotic and change of attitude in voice

JIT: (Mary) We are cleansing the gut.

Ques: You are cleansing the gut now?

JIT: (Mary) Yes.

Ques: What, even mine?

JIT: (Mary) No.

Ques: Are you doing anything to me at the moment?

JIT: (Mary) Not right now.

Pauses

JIT: (Mary) Take it a step further.

pause

JIT: (Mary) Are there any further questions today?

Ques: Who needs to take it one step further, me? Jan?

JIT: (Mary) Jan asked a question earlier and she will understand the answer.

Ques: So do I need to take it one step further?

JIT: (Mary) Jan asked a question earlier and she will understand the answer.

Waits for more questions

Pauses

JIT: (Mary) The eagle has landed and there will be some urgency to continue with the plans of action; the eagle has landed.

Long pauses

JIT: (Mary) Pacific Hotel and I will be there with you.

JIT: (Mary) Monston Green, I will come there too.

Ques: Where is the Pacific Hotel?

JIT: (Mary) You will see.

JIT: (Mary) There will be a love at a wedding.

JIT: (Mary) All the clues will be there in life. You know I like cryptic, let me tell you cryptic. You know I like cryptic and I always show you cryptic. (She liked to do crosswords in the daily newspaper.)

Pauses

Long pause

JIT: (Mary) Living beyond the pool of love creates no dimensional barriers; there was only love and peace and calm in the natural habitat, cerebral, serene and sumptuous.

JIT: (Mary) Allow the divine to guide, allow the divine to link.

JIT: (Mary) Rest and be rested. There are no changes at present; keep with the motivational aspects of your journey.

Voice is low as if she is tired

JIT: (Mary) Marine creatures will be washed ashore, dead. The bellies will be opened and many things will be revealed from the contents of the gut. Blood also will be analysed.

JIT: (Mary) Chernobyl.

JIT's breathing is deep, quick and shallow

JIT: (Mary) There will be clouds of smoke in the sky; clouds of gasses will erupt into the sky.

Disturbed in the trance, JIT begins to breathe in a shallower, agitated way

JIT: (Mary) All will be well.

Ques: Is that volcanoes?

JIT: (Mary) No, gas.

JIT settles a little now and the breathing returns to normal

JIT: (Mary) I have lots of love for those who are embarking on their spiritual journey. I have lots of love for those who will listen to the tools that we have given throughout these meditations.

JIT: (Mary) Throughout the work, throughout the words that have been given to you we look forward to seeing all the people making changes on earth.

JIT: (Mary) We have given many tools and snippets of advice to assist those who wish to live in their soul's purpose; they will and they can from a lot younger age than the aged generations now.

JIT: (Mary) This will in turn lead to more peace on earth and the progression must be made through the generations and will be born into them.

JIT: (Mary) You look forward to working with these people, seeing the energies raised and the connections changed, the diverse precipitations of life's universal molecule environment.

JIT: (Mary) You know my simple life as others saw it.

(Mary talks of her simple life and it was. She passed in 2012 and did not have an automatic washing machine or central heating. She had what she felt she wanted and always stuck to it. When visiting her there was always so much warmth and love that all those material things were never an issue. We played draughts and cards and talked for hours and hours.)

Very soft voice

JIT: (Mary) It was my soul's purpose. Therefore, nothing, no changes and no words would have made me any happier… And I shared those times with you.

Pause

Waits

JIT: (Mary) Are there any questions anyone would like to ask?

Waits

Ques: How do you find your soul's purpose?

JIT: (Mary) By listening to it.

Pause

Very weak now as she speaks

JIT: (Mary) It all comes from within.

Ques: So, is there any truth in soul contracts and soul Akashic records?

JIT: (Mary) Truth?

JIT: (Mary) Everyone has their own truths; everyone has their own beliefs. Who am I to say that their beliefs or labels are wrong or not?

Long pause waiting for the next question

Ques: Is there anything else we need to know for today?

JIT: Are the questions finished for today?

Ques: When you say questions, there are so many but I cannot think what to ask you.

Long pause

JIT: (Mary) I am not ready to return Jan yet.

Mary wants more questions and clearly did not want the session to end

(Opportunity missed.)

Ques: Do you know my name? Are you Mary?

Ignores question

Pause

Quiet voice

JIT: (Mary) I am just going to take her on another little journey which she will remember.

JIT: (Mary) We will be silent.

She takes JIT on a journey and does not speak

JAN: All I can say is, yes I do remember and it was a journey into my future.

A long silence while Jan is taken on a journey

Mary leaves and a new voice comes in

Begins to speak in a very soft, low, nervous voice

JIT: Good afternoon.

Ques: Good afternoon, do you want to speak to me?

JIT: I am a little shy

Ques: Don't be shy. Is there anything I can do to help? Do you need me to help you?

JIT: Let me think.

She needs time to think

She needs space to think

Ques: Are you a child? Are you a boy or girl?

JIT: Girl.

Ques: Why are you shy?

JIT: I am looking for mummy.

Ques: How did you lose your mummy?

JIT: She fell in the water.

Ques: How did she fall in the water?

JIT: She jumped off the bridge.

Ques: Do you know why she jumped off the bridge?

JIT: Because she said she could fly, so I jumped off the bridge too.

Ques: What, after your mum?

Ques: Did you want to jump off the bridge to go with your mum?

JIT: Yes, so we could fly.

Ques: So how did you lose her?

JIT: We went in the water together. Then I could not find her.

It was dark and I saw the bright and she was there, then she had gone again.

Ques: So did you stay in the dark or did you go to the light?

JIT: We both went to the light. Then I lost her in the light.

Ques: Where do you think you are now?

JIT: Where?

She sounded confused on the 'where' question.

JIT: I am just having a look to see if mummy is here. Mummy is not here so I will go and look somewhere else.

Ques: Where else do you think you could look?

JIT: I don't know names, I just look.

Ques: Can you see a path or doorway to go to?

JIT: Black, I see black, I see swirling black.

Ques: Can you see a door or some light that you can move to?

JIT: I am happy in the black, going now.

Ques: Have you found your mum?

JIT: Bye.

JAN:

As I replay the recording and type the dialogue I realise there was so much that could have been asked in the question opportunities.

The little girl so desperately needed her mum and her mum should have been asked if she wanted to come into the session. Because I, as Jan, am in trance I did not hear the words and I couldn't intervene at the time. Now as I recall whilst transcribing, I have asked for her mum to come to me and collect her little girl.

I feel the energies of both of them around me.

I perform a little ceremony to enable the two of them to be joined together in the spirit world. The voice of the little girl changed to be more vibrant and upbeat, and the mother was so grateful.

I have come across lost souls before and it does not take much to send them over or to reunite them with those who have passed before.

As we spoke of the black it was not some sort of dark side as implied, it was just the universal energy colour that I see so much in meditation.

As I type the dialogue, Mary connects with me and I feel she wants to answer the questions that were not asked.

Jan: I asked about the books she mentioned earlier, what books?

Mary: Any books that others have written; it is good to have a point of view but then to move on and have your own is even better. You will notice that those who follow are rarely meeting their soul's purpose. They are always looking for something.

Jan: I asked about her simple life and why she mentioned it?

Mary: It is important to remember the time to be happy is on the inside. Listen to your soul. Speak to your soul and you will have the answers so many desperately seek. Seeking outside of you will not give the answers.

Jan: I asked when and how will I enable people to let go of their boundaries?

Mary: As with everything else, we will guide you to do the work at the right time. You must concentrate on the typing of the book.

Jan: The little girl seemed to be so lonely?

Mary: She was a little lost soul who wanted to be reunited with her mummy, and you did a good job in reuniting them. They are together now and she will live on.

Jan: Ques asked at the end, that she wondered where Grannie Mary was?

Mary: My work with you is of a serious nature, and I will not necessarily be seen as 'Grannie Mary'. I was the voice of this trance as you well know.

JAN:

This session feels complete now. Mary needed to voice through those last few questions and the child to be reunited with mother.

■ ■ ■

Chapter 8

And Finally, Before You Transform

Zoetic Soul is my journey from one trance to another, delving deep into life beyond earthly knowledge with repeated insights into ways we may help ourselves on earth. Impaired choices of now can be altered to accommodate this knowledge from beyond. Thus enabling a more soul inspired life on earth.

We are given the tools to do this, piece them together to create your souls desired purpose.

As the book was revealed, I did at times have thoughts as to why I was put in the path of Ques. What was the purpose of this person? I would ask myself on numerous occasions.

A lack of understanding of what was being spoken, led to a noticeable reluctance to question the voice. For whatever reason, or perhaps being very much guided by what others have taught them, Ques chose not to listen to spirits/divine guidance and their intuition.

Invariably, people often follow what is written by others, and choose to dismiss guidance on what they experience. Sometimes blind to the presented clues. *Zoetic Soul* gives you information to encourage you to think for yourself.

A little story in my life made me realise just how much I allow this to happen and have done for many years. I have rarely conformed, followed or listened to myself over and above the divine guidance that has been given to me.

A few years ago I was guided to visit Greece, Corfu... I had an overwhelming urge to travel from there by bus to Turkey, staying one night in Thessaloniki before boarding the bus the following morning to Istanbul.

Refreshed, I arrived at the bus station traveling with three other people. Two were Turkish and an American accent preceded a tall blonde tanned male. We acknowledged each other.

The American and I were seated either side of the aisle. The journey began and we chatted. He described and shared his amazing experiences in the ocean on a large yacht, with a crew and paying guests. They had visited many of the small Greek islands and the purpose was for bible studies. He was returning to his home state of Southern Carolina, staying in Istanbul for a few nights before continuing his journey home.

We spoke continually about his adventure, the bible's stories and my journey and adventures.

He introduced me to sections of the bible that were pertinent to that day. I told him that I do not follow what someone else has written although I do respect others that do. He asked me about my experiences that justify me saying this.

Two weeks before, I was sitting in a café on the quayside waiting for my moussaka to arrive. I admired the view beyond the sea towards the mountains in the port of Corfu old town.

Intense feelings were becoming almost unbearable. I was agitated and breathless. I really wanted to get up from the table, push it over and run. I wanted to run for my life. I was needing to run from what though?

I made myself settle and knew the spirits around me were trying to show me something. As I looked along the quayside towards the sea beyond to the hills and mountains, I could see soldiers. They had bayonets; their uniform was of black and red.

I remember seeing them in the distance and I knew they were running from danger, to safety. This was so very real to me, to my eyes I was part of this, battle field. With my eyes I could see, with my mind I could hear and with my belly, I felt the pain and desperation of the soldiers.

As the waiter walked towards me, I felt as though he was in my vision. I need him to move. I have to say I was rather rude as he placed my plate of Greek moussaka in front of me. I just wanted to throw it back and I still had a sense of wanting to run. I thanked him and tried to smile, all the time keeping my eyes on the soldiers behind him.

I slowly began to eat the moussaka but had difficulty in swallowing. I could not eat any more. I asked for the bill and looked as he screwed up his face with disgust at the amount of food I had left on my plate. I had to cross the road and pay in the main restaurant. As I stumbled up from my chair, I almost ran. I then had to walk to the bus station to continue this journey to the other side of the island. I hurried, and eventually looked back… the soldiers had gone. The sense of urgency was going and I stood and took a few deep breaths and was thankful that things were turning back to normal for me.

Mr. South Carolina gazed at me and for a moment, I wondered if I should have told him about that adventure. I usually know when it is right to or not. He looked at me, and I asked if he had any experiences like mine. I knew he had, but he declined to speak about them and I could see him locking them away in his mind. I feel I had done what I needed to, to open his mind to looking beyond what he was reading and to listen to himself. The bus stopped and more people began to get on and take their seats, someone beside him and someone beside me. We did not speak again until Istanbul when we wished each other a fond farewell.

Be mindful and allow your soul's passion.

■ ■ ■

Let's Look At What Zoetic Soul Has Shown Us

By connecting to your mind, being mindful and listening to your inner guide will take you to some amazing places. Those places are on your journey of life. As you were born you were a perfect clear consciousness and able to access all.

1. Pre-birth – gave us insight into what we asked for in this life.

2. A to B - change your reactions to enable forward movement and your passion.

3. Suicide - trance sessions confirmed it was their way to go home. Those left on earth were told by different souls, to live their lives.

4. Cut the cords and sever the emotional ties.

"Release yourselves from the restraints that you have put around; only you have done that and your forefathers and mothers. Cut the restraints, cut the shackles and release yourselves."

5. Access to all areas, Quantum leap and gather tools to enable forward movement. **A great improvement or important advance in something.**

6. Death through the tranced voices clearly showed their happiness and no desire to return to that particular earthly body.

7. Meditation to be mindful and travel to access all that will enhance your life.

8. You are always in the right place in your life to accept new experiences. It is your reaction that accelerates or puts on the brakes your life.

9. Insights were given into possible future events.

10. Perspectives were given from various universal platforms and observatories.

11. Spiritual and life healing at its best. Pure universal healing energy.

12. Connecting with Mary for some final insights.

■ ■ ■

"The purpose is doing what you are doing; the purpose is doing the job that isn't the job; that is the purpose, enjoyment, fulfilment and passion."

Creating My Life – Tuesday 6th September

This was the heading I wrote in a new journal.

"Today I am so awake to the possibilities that life offers me. The blinkers are off. The negativity has gone. The weaknesses are no longer there.

The tears have dropped.

I see the creations and creative abundance within me now.

Everyone can see I no longer hide myself or my talents that help people in the universe. Those who choose to connect will have life changing moments forever.

I am here to transform people's thinking patterns.

I am unique and blessed as a gold soul, I have transformed. I can access all areas of the universes' tools.

Today is the start of the rest of my life.

After about three hours I read it back and realised I had written the closing paragraph in *Zoetic Soul*.

Have a blessed life, living your soul's purpose…"

And finally

Proof reading the final proof, is not easy on the eyes. I decided to take a break and watch a documentary on Netflix.

I chose "My Beautiful Broken Brain" About a lady on the road to recovery from a stroke.

The closing words are

"15,000,000 people a year across the globe have a stroke.

*The cause for my stroke was found to have been a **pre-birth malformation** of vessels in my **brain**."*

Trust, and believe.

Jan Mayfield

Zoetic Soul

Coming soon for you…

Workbooks

Meditations

Workshops

Retreats

To keep up to date and access further information or to contact Jan

www.janmayfield.com

www.janpsychicmedium.com

www.askthespiritsandsouls.com

facebook.com Jan Mayfield or Jan Medium Mayfield

YouTube channel is Jan Mayfield
https://www.youtube.com/channel/UCCVYtm5Fuyfna N7Pn__Aviw

Acknowledgements

Embracing my weirdness are my two greatest achievements, daughters Emma and Leanne. I thank you both from the bottom of my love filled heart for listening and being there for me.

Being guided to thank my now friend Anne Franklin and of course her other half, the scrumptious breakfasts, tears, laughter, guidance and trust we have shared over the years.

Eternally grateful to those whom I have connected to on the one to one sessions, enabling the A to B. I am thankful to those who have lost to suicide and were willing for me to connect to them. Thank you.

I acknowledge the three people who released me from the family to enable me to fly solo in MY chosen life path.

I acknowledge Ques in my life for the times of recording the trance sessions and trying to keep up with the voices' need for questions. We were only meant for those sessions and no more.

Angela, my friend, who is the most amazing spiritual person, has given me numerous segments of valuable guidance. Thanking you for our chats, time together and our uniqueness embraced.

∞ ∞ ∞

About the Author

Jan Mayfield, born the black sheep of the family, always seemed to be the butt of peoples' jokes. Although she laughed out loud, inside she wanted to die, hide- away and cry until one day she realised that she wasn't crazy, she was a gifted Psychic, Healer and Medium.

Before coming to the understanding of what she was here to do, Jan conformed undertaking many jobs from a hairdresser to a teacher in Adult Education and finally onto a Management post. However, no matter how hard she tried she never quite felt she fitted in anywhere in life.

Transformation began for Jan, after having been involved in a car accident leaving her severely debilitated for over a year. This was integral to her switching direction to pursue her passion allowing her to close the door on her teaching/management profession and embark on her Soul's purpose.

Over two decades later, she is a successful international direct voice of spirits, (Psychic/Medium) Author and Intuitive Business and Personal Coaching Consultant. Primarily she is Jan.

Determination, rebuilt her life again. This time she realised that it was HER LIFE, the life with the lady and the hundreds of spirits who work with her.

Determination, self-belief, knowing, trust and rewriting the life that she had been conditioned to live brought her to this point. Now, she lives with no regrets.